Visions
The Window to the Supernatural

D1494039

Visions
The Window to the Supernatural

by
Norvel Hayes

Harrison House
Tulsa, Oklahoma

Unless otherwise indicated,
all Scripture quotations are taken from
the *King James Version* of the Bible.

Visions: The Window to the Supernatural
ISBN 0-89274-878-8
Copyright © 1992 by Norvel Hayes
P.O. Box 1379
Cleveland, Tennessee 37311

Published by **Harrison House, Inc.**
P.O. Box 35035
Tulsa, Oklahoma 74153

Contents

Introduction

Visions are God's window to the supernatural. He sends them as the Holy Spirit wills. Yet many Christians today know nothing about them and often are even afraid of them.

The Body of Christ can be blessed mightily through a proper understanding of visions sent from the Lord. Don't miss out on the blessings contained in visions simply because you don't understand what they are, don't know how to deal with them in your personal life, or are afraid they might be from the devil. (You can discern whether visions are from God or from the devil.)

Over the years, the Lord has spoken to me several times in visions. He has also led me, by the ministry of the Holy Spirit, to the scriptures about visions. In the pages of this book, I am sharing with you what I have learned.

Visions have blessed me mightily. They have given me direction and instructions for ministry. They have set me free from bondage. They have warned me of danger.

One time the Lord used a vision to show me that Satan was about to kill my daughter, Zona. Because I was warned supernaturally of what lay ahead, Satan's plans were exposed. Through prayer and intercession, God used me to break the devil's power. Zona is alive today because of a vision given me by the Lord.

The same kind of thing can happen to you if you are open to learn about it. You may be well informed about many things in the Christian life, yet not know anything about visions. If you don't understand visions and don't know what the Bible has to say about them, you probably won't be as open to believe that God may actually speak to you or show you something this way. He may have already given you a vision. If you want to know the truth about it, you've probably already received several visions and didn't pay attention to them because you didn't know what they were. You can be the smartest person in the world, but if you have never been taught anything about the realm of the supernatural and don't recognize, or are unaware, of the ministry of visions, then you won't be sensitive to them in your spirit.

Always remember that unless you respond to something in your spirit, the Holy Ghost cannot help you in that particular area. You may have a great congregation and win a lot of souls for God. But you still may not know anything about visions because you may not have taken the time to go through the Bible and learn what it has to say about these supernatural communications from the Lord. In the Bible the Lord says, **My people are destroyed for lack of knowledge...**(Hos. 4:6). This applies as much to visions as it does to other parts of the Christian life.

But even if you become knowledgeable about what the Bible has to say about visions, there is still no guarantee that you will ever receive a vision. You may never receive a vision from the Lord. Many believers have never had this experience. You don't have to receive visions in order to be a Christian. Although I have received visions, I don't follow after them, looking for them — and neither should you. But I do follow the Lord Who sometimes uses visions and other supernatural means to guide, direct, and inform His children. Some people see quite a few visions. I never have received a lot of visions myself. But the ones I have received changed my whole life.

Visions come suddenly, and usually unexpectedly, as the Holy Spirit wills, not as we will. While we are not to seek after visions and other miraculous signs, we are to be open to receive them. Most Christians won't ever receive very many visions from the Lord. But, if you will believe in them, you'll probably receive at least a few. And to receive them, we need to be informed about them.

If you have been receiving visions for years but have not known what to make of them or what to do about them or if you have never received a vision, I believe that by learning about them and by being receptive to the ministry of the Holy Spirit through them, you can be prepared in case God chooses to bless you in this special way. Study to learn all you can about visions so that you can be open to receive from the Lord what He has for you as He continues to pour out His Spirit on all mankind in these last climactic days.

1
Visions Are Scriptural

1

Visions Are Scriptural

Most people don't put any emphasis at all on visions. But there is a great deal of emphasis on this subject in the Bible, and great respect should be shown for any ministry of the Holy Spirit, including visions.

There's a lot to be learned on this subject. We need to know about the power of visions — what they're for and how they come to us from the Lord. We need to know under what conditions we can expect to receive visions. We also need to know the different types of visions and their characteristics.

Visions are God's window to the supernatural. If we are going to be involved in the Christian ministry at all — especially in full-time ministry — we need to know all we can about this subject. God might want to give us a vision in order for something great to happen in our life or ministry. Our understanding of what is occurring in the spiritual realm will help us to receive and benefit from God's supernatural blessing.

This book was written to edify you about visions and to enlighten the eyes of your understanding. Visions are scriptural. They are also powerful. One vision can deliver a demon-possessed person. One vision from God can bring complete, total deliverance to a human being. One vision from God can provide instructions on how to become rich. By means of a vision, God can show us other people who need our ministry. He can reveal to us whole countries we can reach with His love and grace. He can show us where He wants us to go to act on His behalf.

We need to be able to recognize and distinguish between the different kinds of visions. To do that, we have to study what the Bible says about them.

What Is a Vision?

The definition of a vision is simple: it's "a scene from God."

A vision from God is a scene that God Himself wants us to see. It might be accompanied with words He wants us to hear, or by some other type of sound. The Lord may want to reveal Himself at times in one of these "scenes," or He may choose to show us something about other people.

A vision may contain sounds, lights, action — all kinds of things. Whatever form it may take, just keep in mind that a vision from God is a scene that He wants to be seen by *you* — not by somebody else. A vision is a strictly personal matter between you and God.

A good thing to remember about a vision from the Lord is that nobody else in the world has received that particular vision but you. Just you! God doesn't usually go around showing everyone the same vision. In fact, He probably won't show anybody else in the world what He shows you. Because, many times, a vision has to do only with the person to whom God sends it, or with something specific the Lord wants that individual to know or do.

Types of Visions

An open vision, the highest type of vision anyone can receive from God, is one in which a person is just going about his daily business, when suddenly to his total surprise — with his eyes wide open — he receives a vision from God. Usually this type of vision takes place in broad daylight, while the individual is wide awake and in full command of his senses. It is impossible to predict when an open vision is going to come.

In the ninth chapter of the Book of Acts, verses 3 through nine, Saul of Tarsus was traveling on the road to Damascus to persecute the believers outside Jerusalem. All of a sudden the Lord Himself appeared to Saul and the whole world was affected by the vision that changed him.

Saul saw a bright light, and he also heard a voice. Then, during the three days that followed, he received another vision. With his natural eyesight taken out of the way, he saw a different kind of vision of a man named Ananias coming to him and laying hands on him. (Acts 9:12.)

And when that scene, that vision, that God had given Saul about Ananias actually transpired, Saul (also called Paul) received his sight and was instantly filled with the Holy Ghost.

The Lord is so powerful that all He had to do was manifest Himself to Saul one time, and from that moment on Saul's life was changed forever. In an instant, Saul knew that Jesus Christ is real and alive.

Glory to God for open visions! (Sometimes the vision that Saul had on the road to Damascus is called a spiritual vision — a vision in a person's spirit — lower than the trance vision because physically Saul was blinded and saw Jesus in the spirit.)

The second highest type of vision is a trance vision. In this type vision, the individual suddenly falls into a trance and loses mental contact with the outside world. He is moved out of the natural realm and into the spirit world where he receives a vision from the Lord.

In the eleventh chapter of the Book of Acts, Peter received this kind of vision, and he did something about it.

All believers think that Paul had a great commission from the Lord, which he did. But if Peter had not received a special vision from God, you and I wouldn't even be part of the Body of Christ, because without that vision Peter wouldn't have known that God wanted him to preach the Gospel to the Gentiles. Every time you pass one of the Christian churches in your town, remember that that church is there because Peter received a supernatural vision. That's how important a vision from God is!

Some visions come in the night. (Acts 16:9; 18:9.) They are the most common type. Visions in the night are still perfect and just as important as the other types — they are just the most prevalent. But if we don't know what visions in the night are, we will miss out on them because of our ignorance — because of our lack of knowledge. It's vital that we learn to recognize all forms of this type of personal communication from the Lord. We can be destroyed from lack of knowledge! (Hos. 4:6.)

God may be trying to use a vision in the night to warn of some danger or to guide us! Many people will be given a night vision by God and then get up the next morning and say, ''Do you know what I saw, what I dreamed? Oh well, I guess I just ate the wrong kind of food last night.''

Some people have probably already missed guidance and blessings from God three or four times because the Holy Ghost gave them a vision of what to do, and they didn't do it.

That's just one reason why if you don't know anything about visions, for your own sake as well as the Lord's, you'd better learn!

Visions Are Perfectly Normal!

And it shall come to pass afterward, that I will pour out my spirit upon all flesh; and your sons and your daughters shall prophesy, your old men shall dream dreams, your young men shall see visions:

**And also upon the servants and upon the
handmaids in those days will I pour out my spirit.**
Joel 2:28,29

Some church people might say, "Well, I don't know
about visions . . . that's weird!"

No, it's not weird! If you think visions are weird, then
you're very much mistaken. Visions are not weird, they're
scriptural. They're found throughout the Scriptures, and
nothing in the Bible is weird.

Some people might say, "Well, I sure don't want to
go around following after visions . . . "

But what about Saul? Saul followed visions. He heard
the Lord's voice on the way to Damascus and did exactly
what he was told to do. He followed the Lord's instructions,
and as a result, God changed Saul of Tarsus into Paul the
Apostle.

If you are one of those who think that visions are weird,
then it's no wonder you don't follow them — or receive the
blessings that go with them.

But if you know that visions are scriptural, and that
they come from God, then you should also know that
visions can come from the devil. Of course, I'm sure you
have found that out already, if you've lived on this earth
for very long. A lot of things come from the devil that seem
right. Sometimes he comes as an angel of light. (2 Cor.
11:14.) But if you will study the Bible and put the right
emphasis on visions, they will have their proper place in
your life. You'll know which ones are from God and which
ones aren't, and you'll have balance. You won't be seeking
visions. They'll just happen. You'll never know when
they're coming.

The way to follow God from day to day is by the inward
witness of the Holy Spirit, and by the Word of God. Don't
try to follow God in your everyday walk by relying on

visions, because it's possible to go for 10 years and never get one!

Most Christians, I would say, have received two, three, or four visions in the past and because they have not even known what they were, they couldn't receive the full blessings from God contained in them.

You have the Holy Spirit living inside you, don't you? Would you like for Him to minister to you? Well, He will do so, but the Holy Spirit only ministers according to the orders that He gets from heaven. Jesus will always speak to the Holy Ghost and tell Him what He wants to say to you. Then the Holy Ghost will endeavor to speak to your spirit. But even though the Holy Spirit lives inside you, if you've never been taught certain things in the Bible, the Holy Ghost can't talk to your spirit about those subjects because you're ignorant of those matters. The Spirit can't get the Lord's message across to you, even though He shows you a scene, as in a vision in the night.

When you start to understand how visions operate, you won't keep missing out on the blessings God wants to lead you into. You'll start picking up in your spirit what the Lord wants to say to you in visions.

I know from personal experience that understanding visions can bring great blessings. A single vision can change your life. A vision can set you free. A vision can deliver God's marching orders for your life and ministry. A vision can warn of danger, expose Satan's plots, or bring you revelation from God and supernatural knowledge. A vision can even save your life or the life of a loved one.

No, visions aren't weird — they're scriptural. And they're for today!

2
God Still Speaks Through Visions

2
God Still Speaks Through Visions

The vision that Saul had on the road to Damascus happened suddenly — without any warning. Visions give no warning. They just appear. God used that vision to give Saul his ministry. If you are open to God's Spirit, He may choose to speak to you through visions. They still happen today.

> And Saul, yet breathing out threatenings and slaughter against the disciples of the Lord, went unto the high priest,
>
> And desired of him letters to Damascus to the synagogues, that if he found any of this way, whether they were men or women, he might bring them bound unto Jerusalem.
>
> And as he journeyed, he came near Damascus: and suddenly there shined round about him a light from heaven:
>
> And he fell to the earth, and heard a voice saying unto him, Saul, Saul, why persecutest thou me?
>
> And he said, Who art thou, Lord? And the Lord said, I am Jesus whom thou persecutest: it is hard for thee to kick against the pricks.
>
> And he trembling and astonished said, Lord, what wilt thou have me to do? And the Lord said unto him, Arise, and go into the city, and it shall be told thee what thou must do.
>
> And the men which journeyed with him stood speechless, hearing a voice, but seeing no man.

And Saul arose from the earth; and when his eyes were opened, he saw no man: but they led him by the hand, and brought him into Damascus.

And he was three days without sight, and neither did eat nor drink.

Acts 9:1-9

The vision Saul had on the road to Damascus was an open vision. (As I mentioned before, however, Saul's vision is sometimes categorized as a spiritual vision.) The thing that distinguishes open visions from any other type of vision is that these are visions God gives to a person while his eyes are wide open. An open vision comes to an individual as he is going about his daily business, as Saul was in this passage.

Saul was on his way to Damascus to go after some more Christians, to persecute them. He had a written order, giving him authority to chain up men and women and drag them back to the synagogue in Jerusalem. He was going after them to do just that, but before he could reach his destination, he was suddenly surrounded by a bright light. Out of that light the Lord Jesus began to speak to Saul who fell to the ground, unable to see.

For three days and three nights, Saul remained blind. During that period of time he didn't drink any water or eat any food. Instead, he prayed. While he was praying, he received another vision from God in which he saw a man named Ananias coming in to lay hands on him and restore his sight.

The Vision of Ananias

And there was a certain disciple at Damascus, named Ananias; and to him said the Lord in a vision, Ananias. And he said, Behold, I am here, Lord.

And the Lord said unto him, Arise, and go into the street which is called Straight, and enquire in the house of Judas for one called Saul of Tarsus: for, behold, he prayeth,

And hath seen in a vision a man named Ananias coming in, and putting his hand on him, that he might receive his sight.

Then Ananias answered, Lord, I have heard by many of this man, how much evil he hath done to thy saints at Jerusalem:

And here he hath authority from the chief priests to bind all that call on thy name.

But the Lord said unto him, Go thy way: for he is a chosen vessel unto me, to bear my name before the Gentiles, and kings, and the children of Israel:

For I will shew him how great things he must suffer for my name's sake.

And Ananias went his way, and entered into the house; and putting his hands on him said, Brother Saul, the Lord, even Jesus, that appeared unto thee in the way as thou camest, hath sent me, that thou mightest receive thy sight, and be filled with the Holy Ghost.

And immediately there fell from his eyes as it had been scales: and he received sight forthwith, and arose, and was baptized.

And when he had received meat, he was strengthened. Then was Saul certain days with the disciples which were at Damascus.

And straightway he preached Christ in the synagogues, that he is the Son of God.

Acts 9:10-20

In his second vision, Saul saw a man named Ananias coming in and laying his hands on him to restore his sight.

Ananias had also received a vision in which the Lord had told him what he was to do. He instructed him where to find Saul. He told him to lay hands on him so that Saul's vision would be restored to him, and so he would be filled with the Holy Ghost.

The Lord said, "Saul has already seen you coming and laying your hands on him. He's going to be healed, receive his sight, and be filled with the Holy Spirit."

Ananias didn't want to go. He argued with the Lord a little bit because he knew Saul had been so ruthless. But in the end he obeyed God.

Saul, now known to us as the Apostle Paul, was also obedient to the Lord. After his sight had been restored, and he had been filled with the Holy Spirit, he stayed there in Damascus and began to preach in the Jewish synagogues.

The new apostle didn't waste any time. He started right in preaching the Gospel. If a person stays blind for three days and prays, he can get a lot of revelation from God!

It's amazing what the Lord can teach an individual in three days. Through visions and instruction the Lord taught Paul and gave him his ministry. You could say that before Paul started preaching in the synagogues, he got his full New Testament Bible training course in three days.

God can take you into the spirit, keep you there three days, and teach you more than you can learn by going to Bible school for 700 years.

The Holy Ghost is a great teacher.

Open Visions

Open visions still happen today.

I have had several open visions. In fact, the first vision I ever received from the Lord was an open vision.

Although this is not the first open vision I received from God, I want to tell you about a vision I had concerning Brother Kenneth Hagin and his wife, Oretha, and their ministry. It's a good illustration of how suddenly and

unexpectedly a vision can unfold — and how far-reaching
it can be.

One time I was speaking at a church in Indianapolis,
Indiana. Without my knowing it, Brother and Sister Hagin
came into the meeting. I didn't know they were going to
be there. They just came in and sat down. After the meeting,
the pastor of the church in which I was speaking asked me
to come to his home for some food and fellowship. He asked
me if I would invite the Hagins. I did, and they accepted.
I was sitting there, talking to Oretha Hagin. We were just
having a sweet conversation.

"Well, Brother Norvel," she was saying, "we want to
help other young ministries. We really do."

She began telling me that she and Brother Hagin
wanted to train up 40, 50, or 60 young ministers — chosen
vessels of the Lord.

"We'd just like to train them up in the ways of the Lord.
We can teach them some things the Lord has taught us,
and be a blessing to them."

While Oretha was sitting there telling me all of this,
I was quietly listening to her, with no earthly idea that I
was going to receive anything from the Lord. All of a sudden
I began to receive a vision. I saw a huge campus!

"No, no, it's not going to be like that!" I interrupted
Oretha. At that sudden outburst, her conversation just
disappeared. Then she sat wide-eyed and listened as I began
to speak out what I was seeing in the vision.

"I see a campus," I told her, "a large campus with
hundreds and hundreds of people and lots of buildings."

"Oh no!" she cried, "I thought we were going to get
some rest!"

"No," I told her, "there's no rest for anybody as smart
as you."

In that vision I saw the Rhema Bible Training Center campus in Broken Arrow, Oklahoma. I saw it as clear as day. And what I saw I spoke out. I spoke it forth so powerfully because I saw it so strongly. That was before anything about Rhema had even been started. At that time the Hagins were just thinking about getting one room and inviting in a handful of young ministers at a time. In the vision He gave me, the Lord showed me that was not what He had in mind at all.

You might say, "Now, Brother Norvel, why would Jesus show you the Rhema campus and not show it to Brother and Sister Hagin?"

Are you kidding? In those days, seeing a campus like that would have scared them. It might have scared me if the vision had been about me.

At that time in my life and ministry if the Lord had given me a vision like that — if I had heard God saying, "I'm going to hold you responsible for building that campus . . . you'll have thousands of students . . . it will cost millions of dollars and you're going to build it" — I would have been a nervous wreck. But not now. I have since learned that as God promotes you along in life, things don't make you nervous anymore.

This vision just "blew away" Brother Hagin. You might think he would have been so excited that he would have wanted to build another Rhema somewhere else. Instead he said to me, "Oh no, no! Please don't see another one!"

"No, I don't see another one," I assured him. "But I do see that this one will spread to different areas."

Look at all the campuses the University of Texas has in different towns. The University of Tennessee has several campuses all over the state. Well, this vision I had received was on the same principle. And it has since come to pass. Today there are little "Rhemas" in Africa, India, and other places in the world. And they're set up the same way as the one I was shown by the Lord.

This vision was unique. You don't see graduating classes everywhere like the ones from Rhema. Each year Rhema produces graduates who have the word of faith on the inside of them, and who know how to pray for people to get them healed and how to cast out devils to set people free.

You take a drove of people like that and march them out after they get their diplomas, and you kind of feel sorry for the devil. They don't have any mercy on him. They just go marching into a city, get out of the car, and declare: "Look, Satan, I'm here. I'm from Rhema. In Jesus' name I cast out devils and pray for the sick. I bind you, in Jesus' name. Glory to God. I've been sent here by God Himself to get some of these precious souls into heaven, and you're not going to stop me. Satan, I bind you up in Jesus' name. I'm going to pray for everybody in town who's sick. I'm going to cast you out every time I come into contact with you. I'm going to throw you out, in Jesus' name."

That experience was proof to me that God still speaks to His people through open visions.

More Open Visions

Several years ago, God gave me two open visions within the same week. It was during the annual Campmeeting held by Brother Hagin in Tulsa, Oklahoma. I was one of the scheduled speakers. My eyes were wide open when I had both visions.

The first one involved angels. God had never given me a vision before to show me how He works together with the angels. But you know, angels help God. They're God's helpers. They really are. They help Him do things. We don't even know all the beauties of angels. The angels have a ministry here on earth.

In the vision, I saw people, and angels were working among them, in the spirit. They were giving the people new hearts. I saw the angels just pumping new hearts into people. And I saw that some of the people couldn't stand it. I saw some of them fall flat on the floor as they received their new heart.

The Lord spoke to me and said, "I'll let you know when to act. When I do, tell the people what you saw in the vision before you begin to call the ones down who need a new heart. Tell them what you saw, how that some of them can't stand it, that they will fall flat on the floor. Tell them to yield themselves to Me. Tell them all that in advance, because I will do it. I'm going to do exactly what you saw. Tell them. Then, when I do it, it will build the faith of the ones who are not even saved, and the ones who have one foot in and one foot out. It will build their faith so strongly, they'll know that I'm guiding what is happening and that I can do things for them. And that will show them that I do talk to men and women."

"But Lord," I argued, "I can't do that, I don't have that kind of makeup. Besides, Father, there are about nine or ten thousand people sitting out there. I can't get up in front of all that crowd and say that."

"I'll let you know when," He answered. "Don't do anything until I let you know."

So several nights later I was sitting up there on the platform, along with 40 or 50 other people — because at this Campmeeting, the board of directors was invited to sit on the platform. Brother Hagin was speaking, and the Spirit of God began to move up into me. The Lord said, "Now is the time that I shall give new hearts to people."

I said, "Jesus, Brother Hagin's speaking. I don't want to interrupt him." Then I added, "He knows You, Lord. Speak to him and have him call me."

All of a sudden, about 60 seconds after I had said that to the Lord, Brother Hagin turned around and asked, "Did one of you get something from the Lord?"

"Yes, I did," I answered. I got up in front of that huge crowd and told them what the Lord had told me to say. And it all happened — just as I had seen it in the vision.

The Second Vision

Later that week I received another vision. And the second vision was a real unusual one.

During the course of Campmeeting I was standing on the stage while Brother Hagin was praying for the sick. All of a sudden, he wheeled around and said, "Brother Norvel, come down here and pray for the audience."

So I jumped down off the platform, went over to the front of the stage and started praying for the people who had come forward for prayer. I picked up right where Brother Hagin had left off. By the time I got to the end of the line, three or four people fell at one time, flat on the floor, and I fell on top of them. I felt as though I had gotten healed myself. I didn't even know I was sick.

I started to get up but couldn't. My arms and legs were like rubber. My mind was perfect, but my body wouldn't respond.

"Lift me up," I told the ushers. "Get me to the sick people as quick as you can. I can't get up." They came to lift me up, and I told them, "Get my hands on the sick."

My arms would hardly do anything, but boy, I'm telling you, the healing power of God was in my hands so powerfully that I knew I could just touch somebody and sickness would go! When you've got it that strong, brother, you know it.

After a while, the ushers carried me back to my motel room.

When those two young fellows took me to the motel, they had to carry me through the lobby with my legs dragging behind me and my arms hanging limp at my sides. You should have seen the desk clerk and the people in that lobby! I know what they were thinking: "Boy, he's been on one! I mean, he has really got it good!" And I had been on one. And I did have it good. You'd better believe I had it Holy Ghost good!

My feet wouldn't work, so the young guys dragged me through the lobby and into the elevator, and then from the elevator down the hallway and into my room.

"Just drag me over to that chair, boys," I told them. "I'll sit there for a little while till my feeling starts coming back."

So they bent over and turned me loose. When they did, one of them said, "Ahhh!" and fell over on the bed. The other one started to act like he was drunk; he had to hold onto the wall to keep from falling on his face.

After a while, I went to bed. Boy, what a night's sleep! I woke up the next morning, eyes wide open, just looking straight ahead. Every fiber in my being seemed to be asleep. It was as though the whole world was in slow motion.

Everything was so calm, so peaceful, and I was just staring at the wall. All of a sudden, the wall disappeared, but my eyes were still wide open. As the wall disappeared, in its place I saw a tree — and the tree was full of fruit. I don't know what kind of fruit it was, but I knew it was good fruit.

Then the tree started coming toward me. The tree was far off when I first saw it, as if it was way over on a hill, but then it started moving in my direction. When it got closer, I noticed that all the fruit had fallen off. The limbs were just bare, and the fruit was piled up at the foot of the tree. As it came even closer to me, suddenly I saw that the tree had changed into *me*.

"That's me," I cried, "that's me!"

I looked down at my feet where the fruit was, and I saw that it wasn't fruit at all, it was money. I was standing in a huge pile of cash.

Fruit was falling off of me, and I had received an inner revelation from the Lord. I saw that the Lord was giving me another ministry:

"Now, son, I want you to bear fruit for the Body of Christ. You're going to bear fruit for Rhema. I showed it to you as a campus before it ever got started, and I'm going to use you to bear some fruit so you can see a campus in full as you saw it that day in the vision in Indiana. You will be one who will help bear that fruit. I'll let you know when. . ."

When the wall came back, I was sitting there on my bed, and then I shook my head. I could hardly believe what I had seen.

But the point of it is this: you can't live in a dream world, my brother or sister. I was wide awake and I did see the vision. That's the thing. I did see it. I didn't dream it up, either. I saw it. And I knew it was from God. It was the sweetest, simplest vision in the world.

Two days later, I was in Campmeeting, and the Rhema singers began to sing. I was just sitting there, minding my own business when, all of a sudden, I received the last part of that vision again. I saw myself standing there, with money piled all around me, and the Spirit of God rose up in me again and said, "This is it! This is the time, son. This will be your first mission of your new ministry of bearing fruit for Me."

"Yes, Lord," I said.

When the last song was finished, the Spirit of the Lord said to me, "Right now!"

31

So I got up and announced, "The Lord has said to me that our foreign missionaries who are here from 23 countries are His special guests, and He wants to bear some fruit tonight. He wants to divide up equally among them everything that comes in. So would you please come and give your fruit? Just pile it here, all around me. It's all for the foreign missionaries. God said they're your special guests and you're home folks. You cook a special meal when you invite a guest to come to your home. God said that these people should be treated that same way — like special guests. What does that mean? It means, give to them big!"

The whole audience of five thousand people jumped up out of their seats and started working their way toward the front of the auditorium. When it was all over, they had piled $38,000 around my feet! And every bit of it went to those special guests the Lord had instructed me to tell the people to honor.

That's the ministry of visions. You and I can receive all different kinds of visions, but these I have just related were open visions. I received them, not because I sought them, but simply because I was open to the Spirit of the Lord.

Are you open to God's Spirit? Are you willing to receive visions from the Lord?

3
Visions Bring Powerful Results

3

Visions Bring Powerful Results

One vision sent from God was powerful enough to get thousands of churches built on the earth.

...Peter went up upon the housetop to pray about the sixth hour:

And he became very hungry, and would have eaten: but while they made ready, he fell into a trance,

And saw heaven opened, and a certain vessel descending unto him, as it had been a great sheet knit at the four corners, and let down to the earth:

Wherein were all manner of fourfooted beasts of the earth, and wild beasts, and creeping things, and fowls of the air.

And there came a voice to him, Rise, Peter; kill, and eat.

But Peter said, Not so, Lord; for I have never eaten any thing that is common or unclean.

And the voice spake unto him again the second time, What God hath cleansed, that call not thou common.

This was done thrice: and the vessel was received up again into heaven.

Now while Peter doubted in himself what this vision which he had seen should mean, behold, the men which were sent from Cornelius had made inquiry for Simon's house, and stood before the gate,

And called, and asked whether Simon, which was surnamed Peter, were lodged there.

> **While Peter thought on the vision, the Spirit said unto him, Behold, three men seek thee.**
>
> **Arise therefore, and get thee down, and go with them, doubting nothing: for I have sent them.**
>
> Acts 10:9-20

The second highest type of vision a person can receive from God is a trance vision. In this type vision, the natural senses are suspended. The individual could be in a full trance or in a semi-trance.

In a full trance the person is off in heaven somewhere and doesn't even know anything about this earth. In a semi-trance he knows where he is and what he is doing but only partly. It's as though he has one foot in the spirit world and the other foot on earth. Part of him is in the realm of the spirit and part of him is here.

When this happens to you, this world won't have any meaning to you. Your meaning will be over in the spirit realm. God will then begin to show you a scene. That's the second highest type of vision you can receive.

A Trance Vision
Prepared Peter To Reach the Gentiles

In the tenth chapter of the Book of Acts, we read how Peter received the trance type of vision.

Why did Peter receive this vision? Because God wanted to give it to him to prepare him for an important mission — the taking of the Gospel to the Gentiles. Paul had a great commission from the Lord. But so did Peter. He received it in a vision. Without that vision we Gentiles might not be in the Church of Jesus Christ today.

In that vision, the Lord took away Peter's traditional thinking about observing the Jewish laws about food and removed his fears about mixing with the Gentiles. In those days, a Jew could be killed for just associating with Gentiles. Jews had to observe all the Mosaic laws, especially the laws about food. Those laws would have been hard to keep if Peter was going to be doing all the things necessary to fulfill his ministry calling. The Lord showed Peter that He could make any kind of food clean. And that gave Peter the freedom and the directions he needed to go and preach the Gospel to the Gentiles. It also served to teach him that God is no respector of persons, that no one — even a Gentile — is beyond God's love and grace.

So in a sense every Christian church in the Western world owes its existence to the fact that Peter received a vision from God and was faithful to accept and obey it.

"I thought all this happened because Jesus died on the cross."

Well, that was the ultimate reason for it. But just because Jesus died on the cross is no sign that your cousin is going to get saved. Somebody's going to have to tell your cousin that Jesus loves him.

"Well, God can tell him."

No, God doesn't save people like that.

"But I know God could tell him."

Yes, God *could* tell him. But He's not going to do that Himself because that's not the way He usually operates.

"He could send him an angel . . ."

No, God doesn't save human beings through the ministry of angels. He saves people through words coming out of the mouths of men and women.

That's the way God saves people, through human words. You and I speak. People hear, believe, confess and are saved. (Rom. 10:8-17.) The Lord heals people the same way. He peaches His Word by words coming out of our mouths, by teachers, by people who sit in the offices of the church.

In the eleventh chapter of the Book of Acts we read how an angel came to the house of a Roman centurion named Cornelius and gave him an order. The angel told Cornelius to send some men down to Joppa to call for Peter. The angel said that Peter would come and give Cornelius words whereby he and his household might be saved. (Acts 11:11-14.)

"Well, why didn't the angel just tell Cornelius how to get saved, and save all that journey, and all that trouble?"

Because God has ordained that people do not get saved through angels but through the testimony of other human beings. (1 Cor. 1:21.)

If you happen to be near a place where there are unsaved people, the Lord may give some of them a vision. God may send an angel to them and tell them to call for you to come and preach the Gospel to them, just as He did with Peter and Cornelius.

God has great orders for you to carry out in your life, if you'll stay open enough to accept them, and strong enough to obey them. God can give you an order to go bring joy to someone and to lift somebody out of darkness into His glorious light. But you've got to be open to the moving of the Holy Spirit because, if you're not, how can God give you orders?

Don't expect the Lord to give you any marching orders if every Monday you've got the blues. If you are in that condition, why would God want to send you to a poor soul to minister to him? You may give him some of your blue Mondays! You've got to keep yourself in shape so you can walk into any place the Lord may send you with victory in your mind, victory on your lips, and victory down in your spirit. No defeat!

God doesn't have any defeated days. All of them are good.

A Powerful Message From God

Through means of a vision, God Himself sent Peter to Cornelius's house.

"Well, why didn't God just give Peter an inward witness about going to Cornelius?"

For the same reason you and I sometimes need something stronger than an inward witness. Being a good Jew, Peter probably wouldn't have dared go to another city to the house of a Gentile just on the basis of an inner leading. Peter needed a vision because what he was being called upon to do was a very serious thing. In those days, it was dangerous for a Jew even to enter the house of a Gentile. He could lose his life. In fact, it was an automatic sentence of 39 stripes just for talking to a Gentile.

But, going to a Gentile family, entering their house, and sitting down to fellowship and eat with them — that could mean death for a Jew. So before Peter would get up and travel down to another town to risk his life dealing with a Gentile family, he had to know that it was of God. That's why God gave Peter a vision. Because He knew that visit to the house of Cornelius was something that needed to be done so you and I could be saved.

To emphasize how serious this situation was, notice how some of the devout Jewish believers reacted when they learned what Peter had done:

> **And the apostles and brethren that were in Judea heard that the Gentiles had also received the word of God.**
>
> **And when Peter was come up to Jerusalem, they that were of the circumcision contended with him,**
>
> **Saying, Thou wentest in to men uncircumcised, and didst eat with them.**
>
> **Acts 11:1-3**

39

In other words, they said to Peter, "We love you and we know that you are with God. But why did you do such a thing? We cannot accept this kind of behavior."

Peter's Vision Was Perfect

But Peter rehearsed the matter from the beginning, and expounded it by order unto them, saying,

I was in the city of Joppa praying: and in a trance I saw a vision, A certain vessel descend, as it had been a great sheet, let down from heaven by four corners; and it came even to me:

Upon the which when I had fastened mine eyes, I considered, and saw fourfooted beasts of the earth, and wild beasts, and creeping things, and fowls of the air.

And I heard a voice saying unto me, Arise, Peter; slay and eat.

But I said, Not so, Lord: for nothing common or unclean hath at any time entered into my mouth.

But the voice answered me again from heaven, What God hath cleansed, that call not thou common.

And this was done three times: and all were drawn up again into heaven.

And, behold, immediately there were three men already come unto the house where I was, sent from Caesarea unto me.

Acts 11:4-11

Now in this particular vision, Peter saw a scene, a strange scene, and also heard a voice. Hearing a voice is not part of every vision, but in this vision Peter did hear as well as see.

Notice what he saw. He didn't see people. He saw beasts, fowls of the air, and creeping things. But those things had meaning. Through them God revealed to Peter a vital message about human beings and His love for them.

40

The scene that Peter saw was perfect. Notice verse 10 of this passage. How many times was this vision repeated? Three times. And how many men were sent to bring Peter to Joppa? Three.

Now, if you will read closely what I am about to reveal here it will help change your whole Christian life. If you'll make a long, hard, study of the Bible you will see that any time the number three is used it indicates perfection.

So Peter's vision was perfect. God showed it to him three times. Three men came from the house of Cornelius to get Peter to come tell them about Jesus — three perfect men for a perfect job.

Notice Peter's defense of his actions:

And the spirit bade me go with them, nothing doubting. Moreover these six brethren accompanied me, and we entered into the man's house:

And he shewed us how he had seen an angel in his house, which stood and said unto him, Send men to Joppa, and call for Simon, whose surname is Peter;

Who shall tell thee words, whereby thou and all thy house shall be saved.

Acts 11:12-14

Notice what Peter said here in verse 11: ''. . . these six brethren accompanied me . . .''

Six brethren and Peter made seven. And seven is a spiritual number. Brother, when you've got mission work, you're on a spiritual trip!

Then Peter went on to finish his story:

And as I began to speak, the Holy Ghost fell on them, as on us at the beginning.

Then remembered I the word of the Lord, how that he said, John indeed baptized with water; but ye shall be baptized with the Holy Ghost.

> **Forasmuch then as God gave them the like gift as
> he did unto us, who believed on the Lord Jesus Christ;
> what was I, that I could withstand God?**
>
> **Acts 11:15-17**

Peter's answer to the Jews was this: "The Spirit of the Lord bade me go with these men. I know that I am a Jew. And I know that I wasn't supposed to be at a Gentile's house. But I received a vision from heaven. Three times it was shown to me. I saw it three times, I tell you. And a voice told me that there were three men below who had come to find me, and that I was to go with them. Then seven of us went together to the house of Cornelius. As I opened my mouth and begin to speak to them about Jesus, the Holy Ghost fell on them. All of them. And they received the gift that we received on the day of Pentecost, which was speaking with other tongues as the Spirit gave utterance. So what was I to do? I couldn't disobey the Lord, so I baptized them in water."

That's exactly what happened. And it all started with Peter's trance vision.

How did the Jews react when they heard Peter's testimony?

> **When they heard these things, they held their
> peace, and glorified God, saying, Then hath God also
> to the Gentiles granted repentance unto life.**
>
> **Acts 11:18**

So in the end the Jewish believers began to glorify the Lord because of the perfect vision which the Lord had used to send the glorious Gospel of salvation to the Gentiles.

"People Make God Complicated!"

There are different phases of trances.

If you receive a strong trance vision from the Lord, you will fall into a trance and won't even know where you are. You won't be aware that you're even in this world — and in a sense you won't be. Every part about you except your body will be in another realm.

But then there is what I refer to as a kind of a semi-trance. In a semi-trance, it's as though you're standing on the threshold of two worlds. You have one foot in this world, and one foot in the spirit world. In other words, you know where you are, but you also know what God is showing you in the spirit realm. And you're more out there than you are back here. But you never fall so completely into a trance that you aren't aware of what is going on around you. I've been in that situation several times in my life.

Now God doesn't usually talk to human beings through an audible voice. But one day God came to me while I was in a trance after making a radio broadcast in the church. I was in the sanctuary by myself. And He kept me in that trance for about 45 minutes. If He hadn't kept me in a trance all the time He was dealing with me, I don't think I would have been able to stand it.

In that trance vision, the Lord told me what the problem is with most people. It's really very simple:

"They make Me complicated."

That was a revelation to me. It should be to you too.

"They make Me complicated," He said. "And all I want them to do is to let Me love them."

The Lord showed me that He wants every person in the world to let Him love them — and to let Him *show* them that He loves them.

"Well, if God loves me, He can show me if He wants to."

No, He can't. He has already showed you on the cross that He loves you. Now you have to let Him love you and show you that He loves you through the Scriptures. But of course, if you don't know anything about the Scriptures, then He can't show you He loves you in any specific area of your life, like healing for example.

In general, yes, you know that God loves you. But He wants to show you that He loves you in every area of your life. But for Him to do that, you have to know what He has said in His Word about these specific areas.

When you and I got saved and born again by the Spirit of God, we inherited the abundant life. That means that everything that we'll ever need or want or desire has already been provided for us. Every need. Every want. Every desire. Now it is up to us to appropriate all that by faith. And in order to have faith for the meeting of every need, want, and desire we must *know* that it is God's will that we receive these things. That knowledge comes from the Scriptures. That's why I say that it is through studying the Bible that we allow God to show us that He loves us.

The Lord used a trance vision to reveal this to me, and He will use visions to reveal powerful messages to you if you learn about them and stay open to receive them.

4
Recognize and Learn From Visions

4
Recognize and Learn From Visions

. . . Paul was pressed in the spirit, and testified to the Jews that Jesus was Christ.

And when they opposed themselves, and blasphemed, he shook his raiment, and said unto them, Your blood be upon your own heads; I am clean: from henceforth I will go unto the Gentiles.

Then spake the Lord to Paul *in the night by a vision,* Be not afraid, but speak, and hold not thy peace:

For I am with thee, and no man shall set on thee to hurt thee: for I have much people in this city.

Acts 18:5,6,9,10

In Acts, Chapter 18, we read that the Lord spoke to Paul in the night by a vision. He told the apostle what to do about a serious situation he was facing.

It was dangerous for Paul to leave the Jews and go over to the Gentiles. It is a fearful thing to go against the wishes of a people who may beat you with a whip — or even kill you — just for associating with outsiders. Yet Paul knew that God wanted him to preach the Gospel to the Gentiles, so he went ahead and did it anyway, even though it was risky.

Paul was evidently frightened, because in this vision in the night the Lord told him, "Be not afraid." (Acts 19:9.) That's a good statement to knock the fear out of a person.

And so Paul received courage through a vision in the night.

And he continued there a year and six months, teaching the word of God among them.

Acts 18:11

The Lord wanted Paul to take the truth to the Gentiles so He sent him a vision telling him what to do and giving him the courage and strength to do it.

Always remember this — especially if you are in ministry: don't be afraid of other people or their reactions.

When you go some place to speak or minister, don't worry about who accepts or who rejects your message. That used to worry me, until the Lord set me free. I can't make people believe anything. I can't even make you believe in visions. I can't make you believe that visions are important. That's the reason I have given you these scriptures, to show you that visions are biblical and that through them the Lord speaks to His children to give them wisdom, courage, knowledge, guidance, comfort, strength and power.

God Speaks in the Night by Visions

The kind of vision through which God speaks to people most often is a vision in the night. (See Acts 16:9, Acts 18:9.) You and I call these dreams. But the Lord calls them visions in the night. No matter what this kind of vision is called, in it the Lord comes to a person while he's sleeping and shows him a scene in the nighttime.

If you received a supernatural vision in broad daylight, as Paul did on his way to Damascus, you would know that it was from God. But the Lord can't deal with most human beings like that. His ordinary way to deal with people is by sending them a night vision.

Let's say that you receive a vision in the nighttime. When you wake up, you have to judge that scene. You have to make up your mind either to do something about it or not to do anything about it. If you see something terrible — like murder, a car wreck, an explosion, a robbery, or something horrible like that — you must be open to this being God's way of warning you of what Satan is up to. You can discern whether visions are from God or the devil.

Later, we'll discuss what you can do to pray to keep these destructive events God reveals to you in visions from happening. I don't mean a little bit. They can be changed totally. However, the point I'd like to make here is that when you see something terrible or destructive in a vision — particularly, in a night vision — realize the Lord may be exposing Satan's works to you so that you can do something about them.

"Stay on the Islands and Minister!"

Some time ago I was in Honolulu, and I saw myself in a night vision. That one night vision changed my entire plans for my visit, and as a result God moved mightily in the lives of many people. God used one night vision to redirect my path and to minister to others in need.

On the trip, I had my daughter Zona with me. We had decided to take a little vacation and visit a few foreign countries. Our first stop was Honolulu, where I was scheduled as one of the speakers of the Full Gospel Ministry Convention.

For a month ahead of time, all Zona could talk about was that trip.

"Oh, Daddy, we'll leave Honolulu on Sunday. I want to go to Tokyo as our next stop after Hawaii. I used to study about Japan in school and it was so exciting to me. I want to go to Tokyo."

"Okay, we'll go there next if you want to," I promised her. "We'll decide where we want to go next after Tokyo. We'll just get our tickets from one place to the next."

Zona's heart was set on leaving for Tokyo on the Sunday after the convention was over in Honolulu. Then we had two more weeks to make it to Rome, Hong Kong — wherever else she wanted to go.

"This trip is yours," I told her before we left home. "You've got three weeks off. It doesn't make any difference to me where I go."

When we got to Honolulu, I was scheduled to speak at a noon banquet on Thursday. On Wednesday night — the evening before the banquet — I received a night vision. I saw myself in the vision, and all night long I heard a voice. The voice kept saying to me, "Stay on the islands and minister . . . stay on the islands and minister . . . stay on the islands and minister . . . "

I woke up the next morning and, over on the other bed, I could see that Zona was still sleeping. I sat up and put my feet on the floor. Quietly, I began to pray: "Lord, I don't even know anybody on the islands but I perceive in my spirit, after the night vision You sent to me, that You want me to stay here and minister."

I gave the whole thing to the Lord to work out His way.

When I pray, I tell God I'm available. And that means I'm also available to be flagged down as well as to go on. I'm available for God to change my plans. I don't have any set routine or pattern.

"I just want You to know, Lord, that I'm available," I prayed. And when you tell that to God — and you mean it — He will take you up on it.

Let's say that the Lord tells you to do something that you don't want to do. Instead you want to do your own thing. What should you do in that case? Obey what God gives you. What did God give me in that vision? He gave me a mission: "Stay on the islands and minister."

"Oh God, help my daughter!" I prayed earnestly.

I just sat on the edge of the bed, talking with God about the situation.

"Lord, I know about visions. I know exactly what they are. I know what I received. I received a night vision from You. And I know the devil's not going to tell me to stay on the islands and minister. You know that I've got my daughter along on this trip. But I understand, Lord. This trip doesn't mean anything if I'm not in Your will."

If God tells you He wants you to do something, you'd better do what He says instead of going somewhere to sightsee. That's all we were going to do — go to some different cities and look around.

"Lord, You know Zona's got her heart set on Tokyo," I prayed. "I'm willing to do anything You want me to do, and I'll stay on the islands and minister as long as You like. I just want to be honest with You, Lord. I will do it if I have to. But I'd rather not. In fact, if You want to know the truth about it, I don't have the nerve to tell Zona that we're not going to Tokyo. She's got three weeks off from her job and I don't have the courage to break my promise to her.

"Lord, I love You, and I know You gave me a night vision. You told me exactly what to do. I'm going to cast my cares for Zona over onto You.

"Lord, please do me a favor . . . You tell her."

I received the answer to that prayer by faith, in Jesus' name. And then I got up and went about my business.

God Works Through
Available People

On Thursday at noon, Dean Bishop Kerry came to me at the banquet and said, "Now, Norvel, I know these people want to hear you teach the Bible so I'm only going to speak about 10 minutes. Then I'm going to turn the meeting over to you."

At the luncheon, Dean Bishop Kerry did just what he had said. He talked about 10 or 15 minutes, and then turned the meeting over to me. I stood and started speaking to the audience. Tongues came forth from the congregation, strong and powerful.

Bible teacher Charles Capps was sitting right next to me. I said, "Charles, get up." He got up, and immediately, the Holy Spirit gave him the interpretation: "Yes, My son, it is My perfect will for you to stay on the islands and minister, and you will minister on the islands from one to the other."

Charles started telling me that great things would happen. And while he was doing that, I looked right over at my daughter.

After the service was over, Zona said, "Daddy, that's okay. I love it here, and I want you to stay. I'll stay with you, Daddy."

I said, "Thank You, Jesus!"

About that time, we saw the pastor of the First Assembly of God church. He walked up to me and said, "Brother Hayes, God moved on me as I was sitting in the congregation to offer you my church. So Sunday you can start your ministry there, and stay as many days as you want. The word will spread from my church in Honolulu throughout Hawaii. Doors will open up and God will take you all over the islands."

"All right, Brother," I said. "I'll be at your church."

So I spoke in that church twice on Sunday morning. I also ministered on Sunday afternoon and Sunday evening. Then the next day I got a phone call from a university student who, along with her sister, was under severe attack by the devil.

The caller said, "My sister is nearly dead. She won't live very long — just a few more days, and she'll be gone. I'm about half dead myself. Would you please help us?"

"What's wrong with the two of you?" I asked.

"Well, we've been like this for two years, and we're dying by degrees. I'm a student at the University of Hawaii, and one of my professors made a pass at me. I rejected his advances. He made another pass at me so I told the dean. The dean called the man into his office and talked to him. Then my professor got mad at me because I had gone to the dean. This man is a witchdoctor and he cast a spell on me and my sister. All kinds of supernatural, horrible things began to happen to us. We don't know what to do. My sister is hypnotized, really messed up. Now she's almost dead and I'm bad off. I know you're the only one who can help us."

"You called the right man," I told her. "I'm going to be at a Full Gospel Ministry luncheon tomorrow. Meet me there. Bring your sister with you and after the luncheon, I'll pray for both of you."

After the noon meeting was over, I met the two young ladies. We sat at tables outside and prayed.

"Okay, girls," I told them, "first of all I want you to understand that I don't put up with the devil and his demons."

"But snakes come into us all the time," they cried. "They crawl into us and make our bodies just wrack with pain. And then the snakes go away, leaving our minds all messed up."

"I'm going to pray for you," I said. "And if I pray for you one time, no snake will ever appear to you again. Not one."

"I don't put up with witchdoctors," I told them. "And you're not going to be afraid of this witchdoctor, either. I'm going to break the power of the devil over you, and you're going to renounce those snakes out of you. We're going to get rid of those things right now, in Jesus' name."

I started praying for the one sister, in the name of the Lord Jesus Christ. I meant to pray over both of them, but the Spirit of God hit one of them and she begin to cry and weep. After about five minutes, she began to rejoice.

I broke the power of the devil over the first sister. And then I told her, "Now I want you to help this one also." I told her what to do and we started praying together for her sister. I commanded those evil things to come out of her totally, in Jesus' name. I told the devil, "You're not ever going to appear to these girls again as snakes. I bind you up, in Jesus' name."

Then I ministered healing and comfort to them.

After that experience I began to see why the night vision had come to me. In Hawaii right now there are two girls whose lives were saved on account of one night vision.

To Set at Liberty
Them That Are Bruised

And there were others. Later in the week other individuals took me by the arms and said, "Brother Hayes, could you pray for me? I've been having snakes appear to me for 60 years. Could you help me?"

"They'll never do it to you again," I assured them. I taught them how to bind the devil up in Jesus' name, and make those things leave.

Then, toward the end of the second week, the Lord told me to go to the penitentiary. The Lord told me to tell the inmates about the first time I ever ministered in a prison, when He opened up a man's deaf ear. So I gave them that testimony:

I went to Lewisburg prison to counsel with an inmate there. While I was there, I spoke to the rest of the inmates. I went into a large room, sat on a stool, and the prisoners gathered around me. The prison officials gave me 55 minutes for a question and answer session. I had been in there about 52 or 53 minutes. My time was about up.

Suddenly a man who had been sentenced for bank robbery spoke up.

"You talk like God will do anything!"

"That's exactly what I believe," I assured him, "if you'll only trust Him."

If you're going to minister on university campuses or in prisons, you'd better know God. And you'd better know what you're talking about. Because if you don't, the students and inmates will nail your hide to the wall.

"Can the Jesus you know open up my ear for me?" the man asked.

"Do you want Him to open up your ear for you?"

"Yes!" he said, and stood to his feet.

I prayed for the man one time and then ordered, "You foul deaf spirit, come out of him, in the name of Jesus."

The man fell as if he'd been hit on the back of the head with a hammer. As he went down, I reached out and grabbed him. When I caught him, I just held him there. Not one sound was made. About a minute went by before he broke and began to weep. The other prisoners around the wall said, "God's in this place!"

When I had finished giving that testimony to the inmates in the Honolulu prison, I said to the audience, "If you want the Lord to open up your ears, stand up." I walked over to a boy who had stood up. I put my hands on the sides of his head and said, "In Jesus name, come out of him!" He fell and I caught him. After a minute he broke and began to weep. Both of his ears popped open and his hearing was completely restored to normal.

About that time the chaplain came in and told me, "Mr. Hayes, your time is up. You'll have to go." I turned and walked down that long corridor toward the heavy steel gate. The prisoners came out and began to follow me, saying, "Please come back and help us. We need you to help us."

All these things happened because of one night vision.

Don't Miss God!

Most of the time, people don't put any emphasis at all on night visions.

If God came to you in broad daylight and gave you a vision, you would know it was from the Lord.

If you fell into a trance while you were praying, and God took you into the spirit world and started showing you things, you'd say, "Yes, oh yes, God gave me a vision!"

But the ordinary way — the everyday way, the most common way — to receive a vision from God is in the nighttime while you're asleep. If you don't know the importance of night visions, you won't put any emphasis on your dreams, and you'll run the risk of missing something important from the Lord.

Don't miss God! Be open to receive visions from Him — whatever form they may take.

5
Visions Can Impart Knowledge

5

Visions Can Impart Knowledge

God does not give people visions for them to rest in them. Just to walk around and talk about them for a week or two, and then forget them. In everything He does, God always has a purpose. There are reasons the Lord gives people visions. Sometimes only through a vision can God bring about what He wants to accomplish through His children.

Visions can do lots of things. They can impart knowledge supernaturally. They can expose Satan's plots. They can set people free. God can bless mightily by the giving of a vision.

Visions contain all kinds of power. The glory of God is revealed by the giving and receiving of visions. Through visions, power is made available to the believer to change things in his world.

God will show you a vision when there is something that He wants you to see. What kind of scene will it be? It could be any of a thousand and one different scenes. It could be a scene to show you how to get rich or how to avoid destruction.

Destruction is not the work of the Lord — that's the devil's work. But the Holy Ghost will impart knowledge to you of coming disaster. God, not Satan, will give you a vision of destruction to warn you. By giving you that knowledge in a vision, the Lord is destroying the devil's work. By revealing what the destroyer has in mind, the Lord prepares you to do something about it.

If you receive a vision with a destructive type of scene, ask the Lord to show you what to do to stop that vision from becoming reality. Always remember — the devil is not as smart as God is. You may have thought he is, but he isn't.

You may have been led to believe that Satan is as smart as God because God created him perfect. That is true, he was made perfect.

The Lord also gave Lucifer (Satan) a will, authority, and power. And He gave him permission to go backwards and forwards into the holy mountain of God, freely. He gave him beauty, power and authority in heaven. He had so much beauty, power and authority, in fact, that one-third of the angels chose to listen to him rather than to God.

Some people will listen to anything. They will believe anything they hear. Just let someone get up and start teaching something and they'll believe it. If they don't base their belief on the Bible, they will fall for anything. Why? Because they're ignorant of the truth.

Many people in the East follow pagan religions which have many gods. Some even worship animals. Why? Because they don't know any better. They're ignorant of what the Bible says about the One True God. They worship idols and other such things because they learned it from their parents and relatives. They've been taught that since childhood.

But when a person has been born again by the Holy Spirit, and gets the basics of God on the inside of him, he knows better than these things, because the Bible and the Spirit of the Lord teach him.

We're talking about God's knowledge coming to you in a scene. We're talking about God's knowledge, not human knowledge.

In one vision, God can give you revelation. He can show you one vision that will completely change your life.

I received a vision one night while I was praying at the altar during a service in San Antonio, Texas. In the vision, I saw people running to the altar. While they were there, I reached out and prayed for a dark-haired young woman. When I did, I saw the Spirit of God come on her and her hands went up, supernaturally.

After I had the vision, I continued praying for people. About 30 minutes later, I looked around and there was the dark-haired girl I had seen in the vision. She and her husband were standing at the altar. He was holding a little baby in his arms. Tears were streaming down the girl's face. The Spirit of God spoke to me and said, "I'm giving that young lady the talent to play the organ." I walked over to her husband who was holding the baby, and said, "Sir, the Lord just spoke to me and said He's giving your wife the talent to play the organ."

"Yeah?" he asked.

"Yes, that's right."

That's the first time I'd ever seen anything like that. I went back and kept working with people at the altar. For nearly an hour the young woman stayed in a trance with her eyes closed, tears streaming down her face, her hands held out in front of her. When she came out of the trance, she walked over to the organ and began to play it like a professional musician. That knowledge, that ability to do something she had never done before in her life, came to that young woman directly from the Lord through a vision. Supernatural knowledge and ability can come to you in the same way.

Now I'm going to get right down to where you live. You have to watch people who God blesses through you. Some of them will think a lot of you. That's fine as long as you keep it on the right terms, and of course, this was on the right terms.

After I prayed for that young lady and the Lord gave her such a wonderful gift, she just loved me — that's all. She wasn't "in love" with me. She was in love with her husband. She just loved me with a deep, spiritual love. I believe I could have knocked on her door at three o'clock in the morning and told her I was hungry and she would have cooked me a full-course meal. She and her husband and I became good friends.

Visions Can Set You Free

I received my first vision from God many years ago. It was the highest type of vision, an open vision. I received it in broad daylight, in the middle of the afternoon, with my eyes wide open.

What kind of a vision was it? Well, it was a Bible vision, though I didn't know that until later when the Lord told me. I had to have something like that to set me free.

"Well, were you a Christian?"

Oh yes, I was a Christian. I'd been a believer for about two years. I had given my life to the Lord. But I still needed a change in my life.

Visions will help change you. They'll change your path, if you'll let them.

I had to have a vision to set me free. I was desperate for it. My spirit had been trained one way for years. And when a person's spirit is trained one way for a long time, he becomes set in that pattern.

For example, you can eat breakfast at seven o'clock every morning for 10 years. If something happens one morning to keep you from eating breakfast until eight o'clock, your body will scream from seven till eight: "Where's my breakfast? I want my breakfast!" Why? Because it has been trained to eat at seven. If it has to wait until eight, your body really goes nuts. It's the bondage of the devil.

When I was a boy, my father taught me to work hard. As a result, all my life I would work like a Trojan. I'd get a new job and if I was supposed to be at work at eight o'clock in the morning, I'd be there at six.

The boss would say, "I've never seen anybody like you — where'd you come from?"

"Tennessee."

"Why do you come in at six every morning and start work?"

"Well, I've done this all my life. My father worked for TVA and he owned two farms. He had me work on the farm. Sometimes I'd be in the field by 5:30 in the morning. It just doesn't bother me to be over here at six. I like to. I enjoy getting up early. I'm used to it."

Your spirit is trained like that when you're a child growing up. I know what it is to be in the cotton field, or hay field, or peanut field at 5:30 in the morning, because I was raised that way.

My boss had never seen a worker like me. He thought I was the greatest thing since sliced bread, coming to work so early every day.

"I've never had an employee who came to work at six in the morning."

"You've got one now," I told him.

He started giving me pay raises. He'd call me in the back room and tell me, "You know, I've just never seen a worker like you. I want to give you a raise."

"Mr. Bishop, you don't have to do that. I just come in so early because I'm used to it. I want to keep my area clean and sharp with everything in its place. I want my department to do volume business. So you don't have to give me a raise."

"Oh, but I want to," he'd tell me. "You deserve it."

"Well, whatever you say." So he would raise my salary. He just kept on and on and on, giving me raises. It wasn't very long until the supervisor came by and wanted to make me manager.

"Are you kidding?" I asked him. "I'm only 19 years old."

My spirit had been trained to make money because I was a hard worker. It wasn't long before I was in business for myself. I built my business up to the place that I was making four or five thousand dollars a week. I had a driving spirit in me. I became a slave to my corporation, to making money. I didn't need that much cash, but when you get involved in something like that, you feel that you have to keep it going. The profits kept growing and growing. I didn't need all that money anymore, but I couldn't quit because I was a slave to it. I couldn't get away from it.

The first two years after I was saved, I couldn't settle down. I wanted to be a Christian, and I was trying to help feed the poor and do the things that God wanted me to do. But I still wanted to make money from my business — and I was doing it.

"I'd like to work for You, Lord," I said, "but I've got to make money. It's got a hold on me. Making money is a part of me. I can make a business boom if I put my mind to it. I know I can make investments to make money."

So there I was filled with this driving spirit to make money. I had fought and clawed my way up from making nothing — 25 cents a day — to making four or five thousand dollars a week. I had everything I wanted. My spirit had been trained that way for twelve years. I couldn't get rid of the drive to make money. If my business needed me, I would work from early in the morning until late at night. My dinner would be put in the oven for me. I felt compelled to work like that. I had to do what had to be done. I thought

I was the only one who could do it. So I *had* to do it. I was a slave to my work — literally a slave to it.

I had a drive in me to make money, and more money. I was a slave to dollar marks. I knew I needed help but I didn't know where to go to find it.

I had no earthly idea that the Lord was going to give me a vision. When did I receive my first vision from God? In the middle of the afternoon, sitting in bed, my knees propped up, just reading the words of Jesus as recorded in the sixth chapter of the Book of Matthew:

And why take ye thought for raiment? Consider the lilies of the field, how they grow; they toil not, neither do they spin:

And yet I say unto you, That even Solomon in all his glory was not arrayed like one of these.

Wherefore, if God so clothe the grass of the field, which to day is, and to morrow is cast into the oven, shall he not much more clothe you, O ye of little faith?
Matthew 6:28-30

All of a sudden, the top of my head began to get real warm. It was just as though somebody had put a hot cloth on my head. That warmth began to run right over my head and over my eyes.

When it came over my eyes I went blind, but only in the physical sense. I wasn't really blind. I could see, but I couldn't see anything in this world. And all of a sudden I came out of my body and went up into the air.

There I was, up in the air looking down, and I could see a whole field full of lilies, swaying like in slow motion in the breeze. Back and forth, back and forth. Everything looked so peaceful.

I thought that was the most beautiful thing I'd ever seen. But then I saw something even more beautiful. From where I was up in the air I began to come down right into the field with the thousands of lilies and to focus in on just one perfect lily. My eyes went right down to it, as it came out of the ground on its little stem. That one lily was the most beautiful thing I'd ever seen in my life. God had touched it, and it was so tranquil just coming out of the dirt. It didn't fuss. It didn't fight for life. It was just there, full of peace.

When I got down to the top of that lily that was so beautiful, all of a sudden the scene in the vision changed again. I saw a king's chair sitting there. And it was empty. Around it there were big blocks of gold — billions and billions of dollars worth of gold. And green canker had been running down the gold blocks and had dried. It was the ugliest looking stuff I ever saw.

"You mean pure gold can look ugly?"

Yes, compared to the lily, it looked ugly. The king's chair, the highest position in the world, was empty. That was the coldest-looking, deadest-looking chair you can imagine. A king's chair means nothing without the king in it.

I didn't know the Lord was showing me Solomon's throne, but He was.

Then the Lord let me take a hard look at those gold blocks covered with the green canker. Ugly, wretched-looking stuff — that's what money is without God.

Finally, I began to come back into my body. When I came to, I was sitting on my bed, in Cleveland, Tennessee, in the middle of the afternoon. But when I came back into my body, I was changed. That's how powerful a vision can be. I was changed totally. I was saturated with the peace of God. I had no more ruthless, killer drive in me to try to make millions of dollars. It was all gone.

I had been set free.

Visions Can Expose Satan's Plots

Always remember this — if a vision helps you or others, it's from God.

The devil isn't going to come to you and give you a vision to tell you to help anybody. If it's a good vision, and it's to help people, it's from God.

"What if I see someone die?"

God can be warning you with that vision. God can give even terrible, horrible visions about people dying. Why is that? Because the devil won't let you know in advance what he's going to do — not if you're filled with the Holy Ghost! The devil doesn't want you to know what he's planning. He's always trying to sneak up on your blind side.

Just remember that one of the ways God exposes the work of Satan in the life of a Christian is through visions. He wants the believer to pray about what He shows him, and break the power of the devil.

God can show you a scene in the nighttime while you're asleep. Examine what He shows you. Study the scenes that come to you this way. Some time ago I received a night vision of my daughter, Zona. I've only got one child — one little girl. You know how daddies are. They think their little girls are the greatest thing in the world. In the vision, I saw myself walk into a room and Zona was lying there dead. But I thank God forever, because He extended the life of my child through a night vision by exposing Satan's plot to kill her.

What good is a vision from God to a human being? It can show him things as they are right now. Or it can show him what's going to happen in the future if things are not changed. And unless something is done, it will happen just as the Lord reveals it.

God can expose the devil, and the Holy Ghost can give us victory over anything the enemy has planned for us and our loved ones.

We don't have to let a person die.

Someone may say, "I believe, Brother Norvel, that whatever happens is just God's will."

You've got to be kidding. What are you doing letting the devil sell you an idea like that?

Jesus said that He came to give us life and to give it to us more abundantly. Jesus also said that the devil comes for three reasons — to kill, to steal and to destroy. (John 10:10.)

The devil is a thief and a murderer. He'll steal everything from us — including the lives of those we love most. Jesus said that whatever we bind on earth will be bound in heaven. He also said that whatever we loose on earth will be loosed in heaven. (Matt. 18:18.) If we're not going to bind up anything on earth, God will have to sit there from the beginning of our life until the end of it and not be able do anything about what happens to us.

God does what we do. But if we don't know what to do, then how can we do anything that's valuable?

When I had that vision of Zona dead, I had to remember what to do. I studied the Bible on visions — and on the power of praying in tongues. I'd helped to keep people alive before, by praying in tongues. And I knew that I could do it. But you've got to know that for yourself. Then you've got to do it. You just can't think about it.

So what did I do when I was given this vision of my daughter dying? Well, first of all, I didn't tell Zona what I'd seen. If I had told her, it would have scared her. I didn't tell my daughter that she was going to die.

You may say, "You mean to tell me that you really believe she was actually going to die?"

Exactly. I knew without a shadow of a doubt that she was going to die if things remained as they were.

"But if you knew that, how could you keep it from happening?"

You have to understand the Bible enough to know that death is the enemy of God. Just know that. Death is an evil, foul spirit from hell. Death is from the devil. Read the Bible and you'll find that at the end of time, the last evil spirit on the earth to be doing work against the human race will be the spirit of death. That's the last foul spirit that Jesus will bind up and cast into the lake of fire. (Rev. 20:14.) Then after that spirit is thrown into the lake which burns with fire and brimstone, everything will be turned back to normal again. And the bee won't have anymore sting. And the tiger won't have anymore growl. He'll lie down before us, just like a little kitten. We'll be able to have tigers as our pets — stripes and all.

But until that time we have to contend with and overcome the devil. Satan is a foul spirit and he's strong upon the earth. But you and I don't have to put up with him. He's a thief and a murderer, but we've been given the power to bind him up.

So after I saw that vision of Zona, I bound up the devil and his demons.

I said, "I bind you, spirit of death, in Jesus' name. I command you to turn my daughter loose. You're not going to kill Zona. I'm not going to let you kill her, you foul spirit. In Jesus' name, I break your power and I command you: turn my daughter loose!

"Understand this, spirit of death: you can't kill my daughter. I know you want to, but you can't. You can't, because I say you can't. In Jesus' name, take your hands off of her. She belongs to me and I claim complete victory for her."

If you have any respect at all for night visions, and if you know what the Bible says about them, the first thing you're going to do in a situation like that is break the power of the devil — especially if the vision is a terrible scene. Learn that lesson! Get your vision straight and get your mouth straight, because many Spirit-filled Christians say, "I'm not going to pay any attention to a negative vision. That's just the devil."

It's a vision of the work of hell, yes. But, it's not the devil! It's the Holy Ghost Who is bringing that vision to light. It's the Lord giving His children a night vision to show them what is about to happen, because they belong to Him and because they have a right to know what's coming. It's the Lord showing His children what the devil has in mind for them in the future. And it can be stopped, in Jesus' name. But not if God's children push aside His warning to them saying, "Oh, that's just the devil."

Most Christians would say: "I had a dream last night — I guess I ate too much. I saw my child in a car wreck. I'm not going to pay any attention to it — that's just the devil."

Then the next week, or three months, or four or five years later, that car wreck comes about. Then they remember and say, "You know, I dreamed this was going to happen — and it did!" And if they had known what the Bible says about visions, that accident could have been avoided.

"But my church doesn't know anything about visions."

That doesn't have anything to do with you. You have a right to learn about such things for yourself.

What did I do when I saw Zona dead in the night vision? I confronted the devil. I bound up the spirit of death and gave him orders to take his hands off my daughter — and keep them off.

Just because the Holy Spirit lives inside of you doesn't mean He will come and tell you what to do in a case like mine when I saw my daughter dead. The Holy Ghost didn't tell me what to do in that situation. He showed me my daughter dead. That's the way it was going to be. If my knowledge hadn't been in line with God's Word, I wouldn't have known what to do, and my daughter would be dead today.

The Holy Ghost
Knows What To Do

Likewise the Spirit also helpeth our infirmities: for we know not what we should pray for as we ought: but the Spirit itself maketh intercession for us with groanings which cannot be uttered.

And he that searcheth the hearts knoweth what is the mind of the Spirit, because he maketh intercession for the saints according to the will of God.

Romans 8:26,27

Do you know what the will of God is?

Victory!

That's the will of God. *Victory is always the will of God.*

Who's going to get the will of God for us? Well, we may not get it all the time, because you and I are not that smart about everything. I sure wasn't smart with my daughter. I didn't know what was wrong with her. She looked healthy to me. But I knew there was something wrong because the Lord had revealed it to me in a vision.

If you'll spend time praying in tongues, the Holy Ghost will expose the plans of the devil so you can see what he's up to.

Anything that visits your life and causes you confusion, heartache, sadness, disease, or anything negative is always of the devil. About the only time that misery comes from God is when someone has been called of the Lord to preach

71

and gets miserable because he won't obey the call. That kind of misery can be God trying to get that person to change.

How long did I pray in tongues about Zona's condition? For about a month. Then one day I received a phone call from Zona. She was at the University of Tennessee.

"Daddy, something happened and I had to leave from work at the bank and come up here to be examined at the University of Tennessee hospital. The doctor who examined me looked at my chart and got upset. You should have seen him. He wants me to stay in the hospital for a week.

"Daddy, I feel fine. I don't want to stay in the hospital. What do you want me to do? The doctor is all upset. He says I'm going to die. In fact, he says I should have already been dead!"

"What's wrong, honey?" I asked.

"The potassium level in my body got down so low that the doctor said it was lower than anybody's he has ever examined. He told me that if I hadn't come in for a checkup, one of these days I would have been walking around the bank and just fallen over dead. He said that if I didn't have an exceptionally strong heart I'd already be dead."

Zona was born two months premature. She only weighed four pounds, ten ounces when she was born. After her birth the doctor said, "I don't know if she's going to live or not. She might make it though — she's got a real strong heart." The devil has been trying to kill her ever since. Once he put boils all over her body. He tried to kill her that way. He's done everything he can to take her life.

"Zona, get in that hospital right now," I told her. "I mean today!"

Then, I went on to tell her the truth.

"About a month ago I received a night vision and I saw you dead. I had no earthly idea what the vision was for, or how you were going to die. I didn't see anything about an accident, but I saw you already dead. I've been praying in tongues for a month and I've taken authority over the devil. The doctor is absolutely right — you were going to die. Get into that hospital room right now!''

''But the doctor will have to put needles in my veins and pump potassium into my body,'' she protested. ''It'll take him a week to get my body functioning normally again.''

''Get in that hospital room,'' I told her, ''and I'll come see you tomorrow.''

''Okay, okay, Daddy, whatever you say.''

By my praying in tongues, the Holy Ghost exposed the problem through that doctor, and the Lord provided the solution. The Holy Ghost worked it out so Zona would have to go to the University of Tennessee and be examined. If the Holy Ghost had not worked out that examination, she would have died because nobody would have known anything about her condition.

That's the way it worked. A vision from God, followed by praying in tongues — about 30 days of praying in the spirit — saved my daughter's life.

The Power To Change Things

''You mean that's all you do?''

Yes, that's all you do. If God gives you a vision and you see something bad, remember to bind it up in Jesus' name. Say, ''No, it won't happen like that. I break your power, Satan, in Jesus' name. I break your power and I command you — turn this person loose and let them go free. I claim victory for them in Jesus' name.''

I'll use my case for an example: ''No, Satan, you're not going to kill Zona. I'm not going to let you. In Jesus' name, I claim complete victory for Zona.''

While I was interceding for my daughter, sometimes I'd just walk the floor and pray in tongues. Maybe I'd be riding in my car, and the Lord would remind me of that vision. I'd say, "No, you don't, Satan. I claim complete victory for Zona, in Jesus' name. You can't kill her, Satan."

Just keep on doing that until victory comes. The Bible plainly tells us that the Holy Ghost will get the will of God for us *if* — *if* — He gets to pray. Who gets to pray? The Holy Ghost. He'll work it out, too. He knows exactly how to do it. So just take it from me. Keep on praying in tongues. Don't try to figure it out because you'll mess up if you do that. Just claim victory in Jesus' name. Pray about it in tongues and call it victory. Call the person's name before God, pray in tongues until victory comes. And don't let go.

God sees your faithfulness. God hears your prayers. And He understands and answers the prayer of the Holy Ghost. Satan can't stop those Holy Ghost prayers. The Holy Spirit will get the will of God for the saints every time.

Now if you pray in English all the time, the devil can stop some of your prayers. Sometimes it'll take a long time to get those prayers answered. Demons are here to hinder and even stop your prayers. But when you pray in tongues, the Holy Ghost is smarter than all demons. Demons are not going to stop tongues because the Bible says that the Holy Spirit intercedes for the saints, praying the will of God for them. What's the will of God? Victory in every case is the will of God. It's a part of the abundant life.

But if you're ignorant of these things, if you're not a good student of the Scriptures, you won't know what to do. The Bible says that God's people perish for lack of knowledge. (Hos. 4:6). You'd better take heed to what the Holy Ghost is trying to get across to you through visions and the Scriptures.

The Holy Ghost and I changed the situation about my daughter's death. I'll put it this way: I was the vessel. I had knowledge of the situation and of the value of praying in tongues. But praying in tongues — allowing the Holy Spirit to pray through me — is what did it.

God exposed the plans of the devil. Satan had tried to sneak up on the blind side of Zona and take her life. But I don't care what the devil tries to do, God will always defeat him — if His people will be open enough to listen to Him and faithful enough to obey Him.

Let's say you've got a situation you want to change. I'm telling you right now that the Holy Ghost is smarter than Satan. And He's here to help you. He lives inside of you to provide what you need to live in victory over the enemy.

Jesus loves you. And He lives on the inside of you by the power of the Holy Spirit to help you triumph in every situation of life.

You may have had night visions. Maybe God has shown you terrible scenes. The Lord wants you to pray to stop those things. You don't have to pray to stop them. You can let them remain as they are, if you want to. If you do, then what you saw will happen just as you saw it in the vision.

"Well, maybe somebody else will pray."

No, God showed it to *you*. You're responsible, not somebody else. God doesn't have many people who understand this principle. You can hardly find anybody who understands it because they've never been taught anything about visions.

You've got to make a decision. You've got the power either to pray God from heaven down to earth in manifestation to stop that thing from happening or to not pray and let it take place. If it is to be stopped, you'll have to do it yourself.

Now can you see the value of receiving a vision from God? Can you see how you can be an instrument in changing things? You can't change them alone, but you and the Holy Ghost can.

I don't claim to be any smarter than you are. I don't claim to be a better Christian than you are. You may be a much smarter person and a much better Christian than I am. But, it's the idea of knowing the Bible and obeying what God's Word says that counts.

Take stock of your past. Have you had a negative night vision about anything? If so, remember: it doesn't have to be that way. Change it!

Did you ever get around a person and feel in your spirit that he or she was going to die? Or that something terrible was going to happen to that individual? If you start feeling that same thing two, three, or four times about the same person, it will usually happen just as you have sensed. You can break the power of the devil over that individual. You and the Holy Spirit can change that situation.

Are you willing to change it? Are you willing to pay the price for somebody else? Maybe it's for you. You may have received a vision from God in which you saw yourself dead. Maybe you have seen yourself in a car wreck. If so, you'd better do something about it because weeks, months, even years from now, it might happen if you don't break the power of the devil. Satan's got something planned for you out there to destroy you, but the Holy Ghost is much smarter than he is. He can tell you what the devil plans to do.

I'm going to tell it like it is. There's no cheap way to victory. You're going to have to pay the price to get it. And I'm warning you. If you don't pay the price, you're not going to get it.

I can't change it for you. Neither can anybody else. You're going to have to pray and change it yourself.

6
Visions Can Warn of Danger

6

Visions Can Warn of Danger

Visions can help you. The Lord can let you know that something dangerous is about to happen. The Lord doesn't have to warn you about these things in visions, but that is His normal way of getting these things across to His children.

Remember, the Lord spoke to Paul in a night vision and told him not to be afraid to preach the Gospel in a pagan city. He assured him that no one would set upon him to do him harm. (Acts 18:9, 10.)

Now why would the Lord speak to Paul in a vision at that particular time in his life? Well, because he was in great danger. I'll tell you, the Spirit of God lets you know if you're in danger. And many times, He'll let you know by a vision.

Of course, God's best way and everyday way to lead people is by the inward witness. But you just can't nullify visions, because the New Testament is full of examples of God sending visions to His people. He's still doing it. But to benefit from them, you've got to know how visions operate. You've got to know what the Holy Ghost is trying to say to you.

We have said that a vision is a scene that God wants you to see. God wants you to see it because He loves you and He wants you to be aware of things spiritually. If you don't do anything with what the Lord shows you, it's not God's fault. He showed it to you. But there is a way you can do something about it, if you know what the Bible says.

As we saw before, Jesus said that whatever we bind on earth will be bound in heaven. (Matt. 18:18.) So if it's a work of hell trying to come against you, if it's a demon operating and trying to cause you harm, the Holy Ghost can show you what to do about it. You can bind it up, in Jesus' name. You can come face to face with that evil thing, expose it and put an end to it. Learn this: If you let a demon run rampant for very long, it will drive you up the wall. You need to face that demon, whatever it may be. You need to confront that thing as quick as you can and get rid of it.

It Was Dangerous To
Preach Jesus to the Gentiles

So why did the Lord speak to Paul in a night vision? Because Paul was in danger. In this particular scripture, Paul had just angered the Jews by preaching to them that Jesus is the Christ.

Leaving the Jews, Paul went over and began preaching to the Gentiles. Now that was dangerous in Paul's day. Even telling a Jew that Jesus is the Christ was dangerous. But for a Jew to go over and start preaching to Gentiles, walking with them, fellowshipping with them, eating with them — that was even more dangerous. That was death work. Paul could have gotten killed real easy.

That's why Paul needed a vision from the Lord at that particular time in his life. He needed a vision from Jesus Himself.

Now notice the first three words the Lord said to him and you'll understand the vision and why Paul was there and how he felt on the inside of his spirit: "Be not afraid. . ."

When you're facing that kind of danger, the human part of you is always a little bit afraid, but Jesus told Paul, "Be not afraid, but speak and hold not thy peace."

"Be Not Afraid!"

That's what the Lord told me about casting out devils: be not afraid.

"Son, don't ever stop casting out devils and never be ashamed of it. Many of My chosen vessels will start in that kind of a ministry when they're small, then when they get big and get a lot of the big, rich people in town in their church, they make casting out devils a back room ministry for a few years, and finally they just cut it off all together."

God didn't create back room ministries. The Lord wants us to cast out devils in Jesus' name, on Sunday morning right at the altar, and let the church see it. I don't care if the demons spit up foam on the floor or cause a terrible scene. If someone in that audience has a devil, it needs to be cast out right then and there. And it may take a while. If there is a scheduled guest speaker, I understand the need for some side room ministries in such cases. But some people have side room ministries for all demon cases. That means, my brother or sister, that they're on their way out.

What do I mean when I say they're on their way out? I mean that they're going to lose their spiritual power. They're going to keep fooling around with the Gospel until they get to the point that they'll be so nice, the only thing God can do in their midst is pat them on the back.

God wants His churches to be free. He wants us not to be ashamed of anything. If the devil is messing up somebody, don't be ashamed to help that individual. Reach out and pray for him. With reverence and with power, reach out and pray for that person, rebuking the demon by saying: "In Jesus' name, come out!"

I'm not ashamed to say that. I didn't have to muster up a lot of faith to do it. It just comes naturally to me. In the sixteenth chapter of Mark, verses 15-18, Jesus told His disciples to go into all the world and preach the Gospel to every creature, and to cast out devils, promising them that miraculous signs would follow them. In another place He also said that if we're ashamed of Him on earth, then He'll be ashamed of us when we stand before Him. (Mark 8:38.)

At the top of the list, Jesus' words to a believer are, "In My name I want you to cast out devils."

"But I'm a believer, and I don't cast out devils."

Well, when are you going to get started?

"Me? Let somebody else do that."

No, Mark sixteen is not addressed to somebody else. It is addressed to you. Don't try to put it off on somebody else. Every believer is supposed to preach the Gospel and cast out devils.

Paul cast out devils. He prayed for the sick. Jesus said to him in verse 10 of the eighteenth chapter of Acts: **"For I am with thee, and no man shall set on thee to hurt thee: for I have much people in this city."**

Did Paul do what the Lord commanded him to do? Yes. Verse 11 tells us that . . . **he continued there a year and six months, teaching the word of God among them.**

When you face the devil with the truth, he just backs away because Satan is a coward and a bluff. When you bind him up and face him with the truth, he will back off.

"Danger, Danger!"

I woke up one morning about 5:30 with fear all over me. The Lord was showing me a scene in a night vision. At that time, I owned several restaurants, but the Lord was showing me one specific restaurant called the Oyster Bar. He was bringing it before me in a vision and saying to me, "Danger, danger!"

My eyes popped open. I sat up in bed, with that one restaurant in plain view before me, and a voice repeating in my ear, "Danger, danger!" My heart was beating furiously and my pulse was racing.

What did that vision and message mean? It meant, "Son, you'd better listen to Me." I knew that it meant that my life was at stake, that I had better use supernatural caution, because something dangerous was going to happen at that restaurant. It meant that I had better watch myself. It meant that I had better pray and claim God's protective power around me.

So I immediately got up and called my secretary at her home.

"Mary Lou," I said, "something's going to happen at the Oyster Bar. God woke me up about 5:30 this morning and said to me, 'Danger, danger! Beware, son, danger.' Something's going to happen so I called to let you know. Pray, Mary Lou, pray. Pray that God will protect me."

Then I said to the Lord: "God, let Your power hover around me. Move me today by Your Spirit, Lord. Let me take a step forward when You want me to and flag me down when You want me to be flagged down. Help me, Lord, today. Protect me by Your power, in Jesus' name."

Why did I pray like that? Because the Lord had just given me a vision. Through the Holy Spirit Who lives inside of me, He was warning me that something dangerous was about to happen in that restaurant.

I knew the vision was from the Lord, because the devil was not about to manifest himself and let me know that something dangerous was about to take place at one of my restaurants. The devil is not going to let me know anything like that. That was God letting me know, so I could do something about it.

The devil's not that stupid. He's not going to let you know what he's up to. But the Holy Ghost knows. And He will tell you, if you'll just listen to Him.

So I prayed and asked the Lord to watch over and protect me because I knew there was terrible danger ahead. I asked God for His will to be done in that situation.

At that time, I owned four restaurants in town. Around 1:30 or 2:00 in the afternoon, I had a sudden urge to drive down to the Oyster Bar. I got in my car, and headed for the restaurant. As I topped the hill just before I got to the Oyster Bar, I saw that the place was being held up.

I saw some thieves, and they were in the midst of robbing the place. I remembered what the Holy Ghost had told me: "Danger, caution, danger!" So I just stopped my car. Of course, the thieves knew I was the owner. If they had seen me, it might have scared them. They were making several trips and not only taking money, they were carrying out other things as well, loading them into the back of their vehicle. Suddenly, they saw my car parked up on the hill, so they jumped in their vehicle and took off.

Now I realize that if the Holy Ghost hadn't warned me ahead of time, I might have rushed down there and been shot. The Holy Ghost protected me. He warned me in advance. I didn't know it was going to be a robbery, though. The only thing God told me was, "Danger!" When the Holy Ghost says there's danger, you'd better watch out — there's danger! Listen to what He's telling you.

I had another restaurant 30 miles from my home in Cleveland, Tennessee, in a town called Athens, Tennessee, across the street from Tennessee Western College. One day I was just fooling around in downtown Cleveland when all of a sudden the Lord showed me the restaurant in Athens and said, "Go to Athens to your restaurant, and go now!"

So I did what God told me to do in the vision. I went to my restaurant in Athens. And when I got there, I caught my manager in the midst of robbing me. Can you believe that he'd already carried all the equipment out of the place? He wanted to sell it. So I caught him red-handed and got all my valuable equipment back.

God can show you a vision in the middle of the day. He's been doing that for me for years, just over and over again. How does He do it? Does He talk to me with a voice? Well, sometimes He'll take me into a trance or something and speak to me in an audible voice. But He's only done that four or five times in my life. Usually He just shows me scenes.

God will minister to you with visions in the night. But sometimes He'll give you a vision in broad daylight. If you are open to His Spirit, the Lord will let you see things in the spirit world. He will let you see what is going on in the middle of the day if He wants to. When you've got your spiritual eyes open, you can see what is for real.

Warned of a Demon of Jealousy

God can use any kind of vision to warn you of danger. Remember the girl I told you about who received a supernatural gift from God to play the organ? I had become good friends with that couple. Later the Lord showed me in a night vision that her husband had become jealous of her affection for me.

This happened some time ago. The Lord showed me in a vision in the night that her husband was coming after me with a gun.

This couple and I had been good friends for years. I knew they both thought a lot of me. But I received a dream, and in it I saw this young woman's husband trying to get through a fence or something, and he had a gun in his hand. When I woke up, the spirit of fear was upon me. My heart was beating wildly. Of course, I knew what that dream was. It was the Lord showing me what was about to happen.

Now these people are my close friends. I've eaten at their house many times, and of course every time I go there the young woman always fixes things that I like. She always acts as if she just can't do enough for me. But I began to notice that every time I visited in that home the husband would make this observation three or four times: ''Well, when you're here, Brother Norvel, we just get everything. I mean, my wife just goes all out when you come." He always said it in a nice way. I didn't think anything about it because I knew that his wife loved me because of what I had done for her.

When somebody loves you, you know it. This was a brother and sister kind of love, but obviously it was upsetting to her husband.

Since I know that visions from God are scriptural, and a ministry of the Holy Spirit to let His children know what's going on, I knew better than to ignore this dream. The first thing I did after receiving it — right there in bed — was bind up that foul, jealous demon.

"I bind you up and I command you, turn this young man loose in the name of the Lord Jesus Christ. Let him go free in Jesus' name. You are not going to get in him."

I knew that the young lady wouldn't have told me that anything was wrong, even if she had known. She wouldn't have offended me for anything in the world. She always treated me like a king. So I called and she answered the phone.

"How long has your husband been jealous of me?" I asked her.

"Oh, what do you mean, Brother Norvel?"

"How long?" I asked again. "And why?"

She couldn't figure out how I knew. She started crying and said, "Yes, the devil has gotten to him. The other night he even told me, 'Well, you love him so much, why don't you just leave me and go to him?'" She told me that for the past six months jealousy had been driving her husband crazy.

"I'll call him," I assured her. So I got her husband on the phone and I confronted him with the situation.

"Now you're going to have to get your head screwed on straight," I told him. "I have no romantic affection for your wife — not one ounce. I have never had, and never will have, any feelings for her except as a sister in Christ. I know what's going on, exactly what's happening. You'd better get those thoughts out of your mind once and for all."

"There is nothing between your wife and me," I assured him. "Absolutely nothing. That girl is in love with you, do you understand that? She's in love with you. I don't go out with other men's wives. None of them. That's something God hates. The only thing the Lord hates worse than a man going with another man's wife, or making passes at another man's wife, is worshipping a false god."

"So get that stuff out of your mind," I told him. "That jealous demon will just drive you up the wall. Besides, I'm not like that, and you know it."

"You're right, Brother Norvel."

That one conversation is all it took. That demon of jealousy would have kept driving him, had it not been for one night vision. This young man is basically a nice fellow. In his right mind he would never have done anything wrong. But a demon of jealousy had gotten hold of him. And I wouldn't have known about it except for the night vision.

When God gives you a vision of something terrible like that, you'd better do something about it. You'd better bind that thing up, in Jesus' name, and stop it. Because if you don't, it will cause trouble.

If you have a vision of cancer invading your home, you need to act quickly. If you don't, that foul demon will come into your house, get into some of your relatives and kill them. You have to say, "No, demon of cancer, you can't operate in this house. I curse you, in Jesus' name. Get out of this body and get out of this house. Get off of these premises. In Jesus' name, go!"

And you have to talk like that every day, loud and strong. Smite that thing and curse it in Jesus' name so it can't operate. If you don't take authority over it, that demon will keep spreading and working and finally it will kill the person it has attacked. We have to deal ruthlessly with killer spirits. Jesus said that the devil comes for three reasons — to kill, to steal, and to destroy. (John 10:10.)

Now if you wake up and think you've been having a nightmare because your heart's beating real fast, it may be a vision in the night from the Lord warning you. God probably just showed you a scene. If so, study that scene and break the power of it if danger is involved. Start praying in the spirit, saying no to that demon. And start claiming victory, binding up that devil in Jesus' name.

If you will do all this, that evil scene the Lord has shown you won't take place.

7
Great Ministries
Are Founded by Visions

7

Great Ministries
Are Founded by Visions

And Saul, yet breathing out threatenings and slaughter against the disciples of the Lord, went unto the high priest,

And desired of him letters to Damascus to the synagogues, that if he found any of this way, whether they were men or women, he might bring them bound unto Jerusalem.

And as he journeyed, he came near Damascus: and suddenly there shined round about him a light from heaven:

And he fell to the earth, and heard a voice saying unto him, Saul, Saul, why persecutest thou me?

And he said, Who art thou, Lord? And the Lord said, I am Jesus whom thou persecutest: it is hard for thee to kick against the pricks.

Acts 9:1-4

Great ministries are born through visions. Paul's ministry was born through a vision. So was Peter's ministry to the Gentiles. God gave Paul a vision while he was walking up the road. But Peter was on top of a housetop when he received his vision.

God is still speaking to people and founding ministries today through visions. He may give you a vision to begin a ministry.

One reason God sends visions is to prepare ministers and give them instructions. He shows them where to go and what to do.

A single vision can change your course, as it did with Saul of Tarsus. One vision can have an impact upon untold numbers of lives, when ministers obediently follow the marching orders they receive from God in a vision.

Saul had a vision on the road to Damascus. He saw a bright light and heard a voice. He asked who was speaking to him and was told that it was Jesus.

> **And he trembling and astonished said, Lord, what wilt thou have me to do? And the Lord said unto him, Arise, and go into the city, and *it shall be told thee what thou must do.***
>
> **And the men which journeyed with him stood speechless, hearing a voice, but seeing no man.**
>
> **And Saul arose from the earth; and when his eyes were opened, he saw no man: but they led him by the hand, and brought him into Damascus.**
>
> **And he was three days without sight, and neither did eat nor drink.**
>
> **Acts 9:6-9**

Three days before this event, Saul was a big shot. He was a war lord. He had a written order and a permit to drag men and women around in chains. Then he saw a vision. Suddenly, he was so befuddled, he didn't eat or drink anything for three days. He was blind. But before long he would be launched into one of the greatest ministries of the whole New Testament.

Ananias's Vision

> **And there was a certain disciple at Damascus, named Ananias; and to him said the Lord in a *vision*, Ananias. And he said, Behold, I am here, Lord.**
>
> **Acts 9:10**

See that word, *vision?*

The power of visions is God talking to man. That's the power of visions.

How does God talk to people? People ask me that a lot of times. He talks to them in different ways. He talks to people by the inward witness of the Holy Spirit. He talks to people by the Word. And He talks to people by visions.

The reason the Lord doesn't talk to people today by visions more often than He does is because they don't believe in visions. When they have a vision, they don't even know that it is God trying to get through to them.

Are you willing to take an order from God by a vision? If you're not ready to, and the Lord wants to speak to you that way, you'll miss great blessings by not believing in visions, or by not knowing anything about them, or by not putting any emphasis on them.

Someone may say, "I don't want to be led by visions."

Why not? It's scriptural (as long as you follow after the Lord for guidance and not follow after the visions themselves).

Ananias was willing to take an order from God. He said, "Behold, I am here, Lord." Now listen to the order:

And the Lord said unto him, Arise, and go into the street which is called Straight, and enquire in the house of Judas for one called Saul of Tarsus: for, behold, *he prayeth,*

And hath seen in a vision a man named Ananias coming in, and putting his hand on him, that he might receive his sight.

Acts 9:11,12

God only has one way for a person to make contact with Him, and that's through prayer. If you will pray, God will give you orders. And he might give them to you through visions. He'll do great and mighty things just for you, if you'll just pray.

Even though you may be blind . . . even though you may have lost your position . . . even though you may be befuddled and bewildered . . . if you'll just pray, God will come on the scene. What for? To help you. To bring victory to you.

If you don't know what the will of God is in your life, pray. How are you going to have the will of God done in your life if you don't know what that will is? What are you going to do if you don't know what to do? Every time you don't know what to do, pray in tongues. If you pray a little while, you'll get a little bit of God. If you pray a long time, you'll get a lot of God. That's where it's all at in your Christian walk. It's prayer — especially praying in the Holy Ghost. But, praying in English gets a lot done, too.

Pray. Make contact with God for yourself.

The Lord gave an order to Ananias. Why? Because Saul had had no food and no water for three days, and he was praying. It's important sometimes to fast and pray. Visions are important too. God can show you in one scene what's going to happen in the future.

Jesus had already shown Paul a vision of a man, and He had told him the man's name. He had told him that his name was Ananias, and had showed him coming and laying hands on Saul. Why? Because that is a doctrine of the Church. That's the way blind people receive their sight — by the laying of hands on the eyes.

> **Then Ananias answered, Lord, I have heard by many of this man, how much evil he hath done to thy saints at Jerusalem:**

> **And here he hath authority from the chief priests to bind all that call on thy name.**

But the Lord said unto him, Go thy way: for he is a chosen vessel unto me, to bear my name before the Gentiles, and kings, and the children of Israel:

For I will shew him how great things he must suffer for my name's sake.

And Ananias went his way, and entered into the house; and putting his hands on him said, Brother Saul, the Lord, even Jesus, that appeared unto thee in the way as thou camest, hath sent me, that thou mightest receive thy sight, and be filled with the Holy Ghost.

And immediately there fell from his eyes as it had been scales: and he received sight forthwith, and arose, and was baptized.

And when he had received meat, he was strengthened. Then was Saul certain days with the disciples which were at Damascus.

And straightway he preached Christ in the synagogues, that he is the Son of God.

Acts 9:13-20

Saul — now Paul — didn't waste any time, did he? He just started preaching right away. Visions had launched his ministry.

Paul and Peter Understood Visions

And a vision appeared to Paul in the night; there stood a man of Macedonia, and prayed him, saying, Come over into Macedonia, and help us.

And after he had seen the vision, immediately we endeavoured to go into Macedonia, assuredly gathering that the Lord had called us for to preach the gospel unto them.

Acts 16:9,10

Now Paul knew what visions were. Paul put great emphasis on visions.

Paul received a vision in the night. He saw a man, crying out to him: "Come over into Macedonia and help us." The Bible says that after the vision was over, Paul immediately began to get his team together. He and his helpers tried to go into Macedonia, to preach the Gospel to the Macedonians, because Paul believed that the Lord had sent him there.

If you don't know what visions are, or if you put no emphasis on visions, then you won't act on them. You'll stay home and let the people in Macedonia end up in hell — and it will be your fault. You could have done something to stop that from happening.

When I say that it will be your fault, that's exactly what I mean. When God gives you an order and you don't obey Him, you'll never know the result of that order He gave you, because you refuse to fulfill it.

Paul had made no advance preparations because he had no idea that he was going to Macedonia. He didn't have anything ready. But immediately after receiving the vision, he went into action. He started getting prepared to enter Macedonia and begin ministering to the people there.

Paul's ministry was founded by a vision. God got hold of him as he was walking up the road, on his way to Damascus, when a light came to him in a vision, and also a voice instructing him in what he was to do. Here, years later, Paul is still following the Lord through the Lord's visions and voice.

Peter was another man who heard from God in visions. As we saw before, Peter's ministry to the Gentiles was founded by a trance vision in which the natural senses are suspended and all of a sudden the person finds himself in the spirit world. Peter received that type of vision, as we read in the eleventh chapter of Acts. Like Paul, Peter also did something about what he saw and heard in the vision from God.

Peter understood about visions. He went into action based on what he saw in the vision of the sheet let down from heaven. As a result he reached the Gentile world with the Gospel. And that's what you and I are supposed to do today. If God gives us a vision, He wants us to understand what He's saying in the vision, and then He wants us to do something about it. He wants us to go into action obediently and immediately.

Visions will change you. They'll change your path if you'll let them. When Paul received a vision in the night of a man in Macedonia who asked for his help, Paul changed his plans. He went into Macedonia to preach the Gospel, because he believed that the Lord Jesus had sent him there. Did Jesus appear to him and talk to him, as He did on the road to Damascus, telling him to go to Macedonia? No. This time Paul received his marching orders from the Lord in a vision in the night.

In that vision, Paul saw a man crying out to him: "Come over and help us!"

Today people all over the world are crying out like that to you and to me! Why don't you pray and tell God you're available. See if the Lord won't find enough favor in you to send you to one of those places like Macedonia to preach the Gospel? That would be the greatest promotion you ever got in your life. If you receive a vision, or if a voice speaks to you and tells you to go, you're getting an order directly from God Himself.

As we have said, the usual way for God to lead people is by the inward witness. If you receive a vision, and the vision is from God, you'll have the beautiful freedom of the inward witness to confirm that call. If God tells you to go to Germany, every time somebody says "Germany," the Holy Ghost will just give you the witness. You'll feel so good down in your spirit, you'll know that your call and ministry have been confirmed by the Lord.

It's Still Happening Today

God gave a vision to a person I know. When she was 17, she received a vision while she was praying. The Lord told her to go to a certain city, start preaching and build a church for Him there. The Lord confirmed the call by revealing to her mother in a vision what He had shown the daughter. This teenaged girl didn't have any money and neither did her mother. But that didn't stop either of them from being obedient to what God had revealed to them in visions.

God told the mother to go with her daughter to back her up and help her: "I have called your daughter to go to a certain city and build a church there for Me. You are to go with her and help her in every way you can."

So this young woman told her mother about the vision. Her mother said, "I already know it. I'll go with you."

"But, Mama," the girl answered. "I'm going to have to preach."

Many people would have argued, "Preach? But daughter, the people you're going to don't even believe in women preachers!"

But not this mother. She knew that it's not what people believe that's important, it's what God says. That's what counts. It's not what our friends believe, and not what we believe either. It's what God says that matters. If God wants to call a 17-year-old girl to preach, God can call a 17-year-old girl to preach.

So the Lord called this girl to pack up and move to another town and build a church for Him. And because she believed in what her daughter was doing, the mother went with her. They had no money, no building, and they didn't know anybody in town. They found a vacant lot on the outskirts of the city. They got permission from the man who owned the lot to preach out in the field, and they just went out and started pulling up weeds.

For days, they worked out there with their bare hands. They pulled up the weeds to get a clear spot to put about 15 or 20 seats and a little riser so the girl could stand on it and preach.

One day a pastor happened to drive by. He stopped, and asked, "What are you ladies doing?"

"We're pulling up weeds. We're going to put up some seats and hold church services."

"Who's going to preach?"

The 17-year-old girl said, "I am."

"You're going to preach?"

"Yes, the Lord told me to come here and preach and build a church."

That wouldn't have gone over very well with some pastors, especially back in those days. But this minister was filled with God, and was not jealous of another church coming into his area. He was certainly not jealous of a 17-year-old girl.

"What are you going to use for music?" he asked.

"We don't have anything to use. We could play a piano . . ."

"I'm the pastor of the Assembly of God church here in town," he remarked.

"Well," said the girl boldly, "We'd have a piano if you'd loan us yours!"

"Loan you mine? From the church? I can't loan you my piano from the church. It would be out here under the sky at night. The dew would fall on it. It would ruin it."

"Well, I'd have a little shed to put over it — if you'd build me one."

By this time the pastor was wondering, "What did I stop here for? This 17-year-old-girl is something else!"

Finally he said, "Well, I've got some carpenters in the church. Let me go see if I can round up two or three of them to come out here and build you a little platform and shed. If I can, I'll loan you the piano."

"Oh, thank You, Lord!" said the girl as he left. And she and her mother just kept pulling up weeds.

The ladies managed to get a few things — logs, cartons, blocks of wood — anything they could find to put out there in that empty field for people to sit on. Then they invited people to "come to church."

"We don't have any chairs, but we have a stump over here you can sit on . . ."

And so the girl started preaching. The first night, there were eight people there. The second night there were about 12 people, and the third night about 15. She preached every night for several days.

It wasn't very long until a family came with a little boy. He got saved. The mother got saved. The father got saved. The mother went and got her sister, and her sister and her husband and their little boy came. They all got saved. They went and got another sister. And she and her husband and their little boy came. All six parents got saved, and all three boys got saved. And God gave all three boys the same kind of musical talent.

The three little boys were Mickey Gilley, Jerry Lee Lewis, and Jimmy Swaggart. In spite of the disappointing controversy in the latter part of Jimmy's life, it's obvious that he has reached thousands with the ministry of salvation.

And how did all of that come about? By a vision God sent to a 17-year-old girl.

While she was praying, the voice of the Lord came to her and instructed her to go to a certain town and preach there and build a church. And she obeyed. She built the church. As far as I know, the church is still there. She started getting people saved, that little girl did, and she just kept on getting them saved.

She told me, "All during that meeting, after Jimmy got saved, he was running around saying, 'I'm going to be a preacher.' He was eight years old, and saying, 'When I get big, I'm going to preach like that girl!'"

And he told the truth.

God Has a Mission for You!

Now you might say, "Why didn't God pick a famous evangelist to go there?" A famous evangelist wouldn't have been the right person to get the job done. The 17-year-old girl was more effective in this particular case.

I don't care what you look like. I don't care where you come from. In this life, God's got a mission for you. Pray and find out where the Lord wants you to go.

And don't worry about what anyone else is doing. Don't worry about your friend building a big church with a thousand people while you haven't even started one yet. Put that out of your mind. Pray for him. If he's got a thousand people in his church, that's good. God can send you on one missionary trip, and by the results of that one trip, through one vision, he can get more people to come into the Kingdom of God than 25 nationally known evangelists can get in a year. That's on one mission trip!

Do you want me to tell you who that girl was? You may not know her, but you probably know of the family. She was Lester Sumrall's sister, Leona Sumrall Murphy. She and her husband are now involved in Brother Sumrall's television ministry, praying for people every night. And she still preaches.

Because she obeyed God as a 17-year-old girl, thousands of souls were saved. Between her own ministry and the ministry of Jimmy Swaggart, who was saved under her preaching at the age of eight, hundreds of thousands of souls have been won to Jesus. That's how important one single vision from God can be.

Pray that God will give you a vision as the Holy Spirit wills. Maybe there is some little bright boy on the street somewhere who's got needle marks in his arms and nobody loves him. The Lord may want you to put your arms around him and love him and get his young body cleansed, healed, and filled with the Spirit of God. Maybe he'll wind up being the biggest evangelist in America. Maybe he'll bring in thousands of souls — and look at the reward you'll get!

Pray. Pray that God will give you a vision — a vision for ministry. Pray that the Lord will lead you by His Spirit. Pray that He will show you where He wants *you* to go and what He wants *you* to do.

8
The Importance of a Personal Vision

8

The Importance of a Personal Vision

When my wife and I separated, she told me, "Norvel, I've lived with you for 11 years, and I've got more respect for you than any man I've ever met in my life."

"But," she said, "I'm not going to give up my social world. I know you've got the call of God on you. I've known it for years. But that's not for me, I'm leaving."

You see, she knew I had a personal vision from God for my ministry.

Personal vision is important. The Bible says, **Where there is no vision, the people perish . . .** (Prov. 29:18).

The Lord came and sat with me in my car for an hour and a half. He talked to me about my ministry. He gave me a personal vision for my ministry then. When you have an encounter like that with the Lord, you've got to give your total life to Him or die. I'd been shoving Him off for four or five years, and I had no choice. I knew that if I remained the way I was, I was going to die — because a person can reject God for just so long, and then something has to give.

So I surrendered completely to the Lord. That's when my wife told me, "I'm not going to give up my social world." I understood.

She was raised in a social family, in Boston and New York. She was a socialite. Every time she walked out of the house, she always wore a hat, gloves and high heels. That's just the way she was brought up to dress and behave. And I have a certain amount of respect for that. She was a classy girl, and exceptionally beautiful. She looked like Elizabeth Taylor.

I remember how we first met. I walked into this place in New York, and she just fell for me. After our first date, she went home and told her family, "Today I met the man I'm going to marry."

We were married for 11 years and had one child. And it was sweet. I'll have to admit that ours was a sweet marriage.

But when Jesus came and sat in the car with me for an hour and a half, the old Norvel Hayes died. And when Jesus left, I was a brand new man.

I had a new vision. I saw the world going to hell. And I had to do something about it.

When I walked into the house after I had received that vision, my wife hardly knew me.

"What's happened to you?" she asked.

"You wouldn't believe it," I said. "I don't even believe it myself. Jesus came and sat in the car with me for one and a half hours. I'm giving my life totally to Him from this day forward," I told my wife, "and I'm going to seek His face."

That's when she told me, "Now, Norvel, I'm not going to give up my social world."

That's why I wound up the way I am now. My wife left me and filed for a divorce. I didn't have anything to do with it.

It's one thing to give your heart to God, and it's another thing to give your life to the Lord. When you belong to Him, He has a right to move upon you, and to say to you, "I want you to go to a certain place. Somebody there is going to die, and I want you to break the power of the devil over that person. I want you to reach out, in My name. Go there . . ."

If your life belongs to the Lord, you'll obey. If you'll obey Him, He'll give you orders. And how sweet it is! He'll lead you into missionary work. God will bless your life so much, you will wonder where all the blessings are coming from.

"Go Cast the Devil Out of Her!"

Just one vision from the Lord can cause thousands of people to get saved. You could respond to one vision from the Lord, telling you to go somewhere and minister for Him, and your obedience could cause a hundred thousand people to go to heaven. In the same way, if you didn't go, there could be thousands who would go to hell.

Sometimes you may be at a place, or in a position, where God can tell you to do something that nobody else can do. You may be the only person at that particular time and place who can do what needs to be done.

When Lester Sumrall was in the Philippines several years ago, there was a young prostitute who had the whole city of Manila in fear. She would scream out. The devils would speak through her. She told a doctor, "You'll die!" He died the next day. She told the jailer that he would die. Two days later he was dead.

The mayor of the city was upset because that girl was so powerful. She could pronounce death on somebody and he would die.

Brother Sumrall was in the Philippines to build a church. He was shaving one morning when he heard the girl's screams coming over the radio. Her story received national publicity and had the whole city of Manila in terror. The girl told how two devils came to her and bit her and left teeth marks on her. She said one was big and one was little. Nobody wanted to have anything to do with her because they were afraid of her.

When Brother Sumrall heard the girl's screams, the Lord said to him: "I want you to go cast the devil out of her!"

Brother Sumrall didn't want to go, but God assured him that He had no one else to send.

Brother Sumrall said, "I'll do it."

He got permission from the mayor to go into the jail to pray for the girl. When he showed up to pray for her, a hundred reporters were there. They were from all over the world — Paris, London, just everywhere.

Brother Sumrall said, "I didn't want an audience like this. I thought I was just going in there to pray for her myself."

But one of the reporters spoke up and said, "Look, Reverend Sumrall, if you can help that girl, then you're the only one around here who can do it. And that's news. Big news. We have every right to see it, and we have every right to print it."

So Brother Sumrall agreed: "You're right. I was wrong. The things of God aren't hid under a bushel. You have a right to see it. The whole world has a right to see it. It will happen, you will see it and report it, and Jesus will get the glory."

Brother Sumrall prayed and fasted. He made several trips just to get through the obstacles of getting permission to see the girl. He confronted the devil in her and prayed for her. Finally, she was free! The girl received Jesus as Lord. Brother Sumrall told her that the devils might try to return but that she should resist them in the name of Jesus.

The point is that the Lord told Brother Sumrall that he was the only one in the city of Manila who could do that job for Him.

You'll probably be in a position like that some time before you die. Unless you obey God — unless you do what the Lord wants you to do — it won't get done. And one of the ways God will tell you what to do is through visions.

Find Out What
God Wants You to Do — And Do It!

A personal vision for ministry will keep you on track with God's plans for your life. He'll give you a personal vision so you can know and fulfill those plans.

I once received a vision from God in the middle of the day. It was while I was at my mission down in Florida.

I was going to catch a plane from Gainesville, Florida, which is about 60 miles away from the mission. Some fellow came by to pick me up at my room, and he put my luggage in the trunk of the car. I got in the passenger side, and we pulled up to the mission. The Florida mission sits on the side of Highway 79, right on the west coast. The mission's only about two or three blocks from the water. Just as soon as the driver pulled up in front of the door, the Spirit of the Lord came upon me and God gave me a vision in the middle of the day, just as I was sitting there.

This was something else! God left that vision on me for about 30 minutes. I was partly in the world and partly out, and during the entire time, the Lord just kept bringing children before me.

God will give you all kinds of visions. Visions from the Holy Spirit can be a great ministry to you, if you will start recognizing them. A vision can let you know that somebody's in danger. A vision can show you about a shady business deal. A vision can show you that somebody's robbing you right then, and if you'll obey God, you can catch the thieves. A vision can show you the revival coming to the earth. But now the Lord was showing me a vision of nothing but children . . . little hungry children . . . little children with no home.

I knew I was in the car, but I was off somewhere else too. The outside world had no meaning to me. I had no interest in what was going on around me, because I was receiving a vision from God. I was seeing from my spirit, down in my belly.

Jesus said, "Out of your belly shall flow rivers of living water." (John 7:38.) So if you haven't been drinking from that living water that's flowing out of you, ask the Lord to give you a drink. Say, "Lord, let the rivers of living water flow out of my belly." Just talk to Him like that.

The Lord said that those who hunger and thirst after righteousness will be filled. (Matt. 5:6.) Tell Him you're getting hungry. Show Him you're getting hungry. He said that those who seek after Him will find Him and that He is a rewarder of those who diligently seek Him. (Heb. 11:6.) But make sure you're seeking Him scripturally.

Living waters flowing from your belly is scriptural. And it's all free. And you need it, my brother or sister. To live in this world, you need it.

Out of the fountain of living waters, the Lord gave me a personal vision for children. He brought hungry children before me. He held *me* responsible for them. He held me responsible, not somebody else.

So I told Him, "All right, Lord. I have received this vision from You, but You'll have to show me and help me. Let me know what You want me to do."

About a year went by, and I received nothing more about the vision. Learn to have patience. Get your spirit and your faith possessed with patience. If you don't, you'll mess up. Tell the Lord that you'll do whatever He wants you to do. Then wait on God. Don't go out and dream something up. Don't go out and take every vision and run with it right now. God has His timetable. Wait on Him to show you the way.

Care about visions. But don't grab a vision and start following it unless the Lord shows you where He wants you to go and what He wants you to do when you get there. Then, once He has done that, go there as quickly as you can. Be like Paul. As soon as you receive a vision from the Lord, start making arrangements to go and fulfill it.

I was in Springfield, Missouri, speaking at a convention. About a thousand people were there. A person in the audience had suffered a nervous breakdown. The Lord had me pray for this person, and He healed that individual totally.

God was performing miracles and doing all kinds of good things at the front of that congregation. When I got through ministering at the altar, I walked back up on the stage and all of a sudden tongues came forth. The interpretation came, and the message was for me: "Listen, I haven't forgotten about the little children. Yes, I'm going to require you to erect a building for Me for little children. But not now. I'll show you when . . . "

I said, "Thank You, Lord."

Then a year later at Brother Kenneth Hagin's annual Campmeeting in Tulsa, I received another manifestation. One night during the meetings Brother Hagin was speaking, and the moment he began to give the invitation, I knew that the Spirit of God wanted me to leave. That rarely happens to me. But that night it did. The Lord made it clear to me that He wanted me to leave the service. So I walked outside, got in the car, and the spirit of intercession hit me. I wound up going to someone's home and praying with some other people. The spirit of intercession hit all of us. We were on the floor, flat on our faces, praying in tongues. After we had made intercession for quite a long time, tongues came forth. Another person crawled across the floor, under the supernatural power of God, put his face on top of my feet and started giving the interpretation, weeping. When that happened, the love of God came over me like a wave.

Do you know what the Lord told me? He said, "I've watched you. I know what's happened to you. I've watched your faithfulness. I know what you've been doing. I know what you lost. I know what you gave up. I know you've lost the atmosphere and the love of a family for the Gospel's sake. Yes, son, I've been watching you all these years, and all of the finer love that you've been robbed of for the past 20 years — the love that the cankerworm has eaten away from you — I'm going to restore to you through these little children. They will love you and love you and love you."

When I heard that, I was just saturated with the love of God.

Then the Lord said to me, "I will not visit you again concerning this ministry until I get ready. The next time I visit you, it will be in the nighttime, and I will come and show you what to do, and where to put the orphanage. I will tell you in fine detail what to do. I will come to you when I'm ready in the nighttime and I will show you."

That vision hasn't been sent to me yet, but I'm expecting it. And when it comes, I know the plans for the orphanage the Lord wants me to build for Him will all fall into place.

I don't care what you give up for the sake of the Gospel, the Lord will restore it to you. You're not going to sacrifice anything. It will all be returned to you.

I really would have liked to have kept my family, because I had a good, decent family. I had a pretty wife who was sweet to me. I would have liked to have kept her. But there was no way. She didn't want to associate with God's people. She was too much of a socialite ever to give up her world of rich parties, country clubs, and all that kind of thing.

But after I fell on my knees and gave my life to God, the Lord came and sat in the car with me for an hour and a half, and talked to me. When He left, everything in me had been burned out, and I knew I had no choice. It was either give my life to God, or die. So I gave my life to Him, not just my heart.

The Lord told me He didn't want me to go to Bible school. He wanted to train me. He said, "I want to train you Myself. I trained Paul, I trained John the Baptist, and I want to train you. You're just one of these people I want to train, son."

It's God's will for most people to go to Bible school, but it wasn't God's will for me to go to one, even though the Lord told me to start a Bible school myself.

9
How To Keep Your Vision Alive

9

How To Keep Your Vision Alive

Do you have a vision for ministry? Has the Lord sent a vision just for you?

The Bible tells us to . . .

> . . . Write the vision, and make it plain upon tables, that he may run that readeth it.
>
> For the vision is yet for an appointed time, but at the end it shall speak, and not lie: though it tarry, wait for it; because it will surely come, it will not tarry.
>
> **Habakkuk 2:2,3**

The Holy Spirit doesn't make any mistakes. He knows all about you. He knows what it's going to take for God to fulfill through you the vision He has given you. He knows what it's going to take to keep your vision alive.

I've already explained how you can begin to understand visions from God in the light of the Scriptures. I've explained how you can change things when God reveals to you in a vision something terrible that is about to happen. Now I would like to share some things with you that will help you keep your personal vision from God alive.

Build Yourself Up
by Praying in Tongues

> But ye, beloved, building up yourselves on your most holy faith, praying in the Holy Ghost.
>
> **Jude 20**

You need to keep your own faith built up. How do you keep your own faith built up? You do it by praying in the Holy Ghost.

Pray in tongues every day. How much? I don't know. I usually pray in tongues all day. You can pray in tongues walking down the hallway. You can pray in tongues while you're riding in the car. Pray in the Holy Ghost when you get up in the morning, on the way to work, every chance you get.

You might say, "I know, but when I get up in the morning, I don't feel like praying in the Holy Ghost . . ." Have you got a scripture to cover that? Are you supposed to pray in the Holy Ghost only when you feel like it?

Praying is hard work sometimes. You may never feel like praying. You have to make yourself pray. You have to make yourself pray to keep yourself built up. Make yourself do it. It's just like passing out tracts. You have to make yourself pass out tracts. You have to make yourself knock on doors. Why? Because nobody ever wants to do it.

You're a human being and you live in a natural body. And the natural part of you will talk you out of believing the Bible. Circumstances will also talk you out of believing the Bible. You can only believe the Bible one way, and that's by accepting it totally as it is written, by faith.

Next, Add Patience to Your Faith

Then be totally possessed with patience.

You have to be consumed with patience from the top of your head to the bottom of your feet, or you won't be able to believe the Bible all the time. Your natural mind will come into operation so strong it will make you wonder why what you're praying for doesn't happen or question if it's ever going to happen. You will begin to think that maybe God doesn't want you to have it. You will start asking yourself, "What have I done to cause me not to get what

I ask for in prayer?'' On and on you will go down the line, sinking deeper and deeper into doubt and confusion. If you're not possessed with patience, those things will bombard you so strongly, they'll just talk you out of your faith.

You must learn to get patience down in your spirit, if you want to receive the best that God has for you. And live in success. And live in strength. And live in love. And live in power. And live in compassion.

You must learn to have your spirit possessed with patience. Faith won't work for you without it. It'll only work for you in part. Without patience, faith will only work for you sometimes. Many people wonder why their faith works at some times, but it doesn't work at other times. It's because they've got a strong foundation of spiritual and scriptural knowledge in some areas and little or no foundation in others.

The same is true of you. If you believe God without the Bible, you've messed up because God is a Spirit and the Spirit and the Word agree. If you don't have the foundation of God's Word on the inside of your spirit so you can have patience in that particular area, you won't be able to believe God. The Lord won't be able to give you what you ask because He is Spirit, and the Spirit and the Word agree. If you're trying to believe God for something and you don't have the foundation of the Word working on the inside of you, you won't be able to get it because the Holy Spirit cannot agree with that type of general believing.

How do you keep your spirit strong enough that you can actually believe the Bible and operate in full faith and patience? You have to build up your spirit on the most holy things of God. God's Word is holy. Your faith must also be holy, or it will not work. If your spirit is weak and you are trying to build it up on your faith which is also weak, then you can't receive. That doesn't mean that you're not a good Christian. It just means that your faith is weak in that particular area.

You've got to pray in tongues. If you're not going to pray in tongues, you're not going to keep your spirit built up to the point you can receive those things you ask in prayer.

You're responsible to build yourself up. If you don't pray in the Holy Ghost, your spirit will be so weak, you won't accept things by faith. You won't be able to believe by faith with no feelings involved and to speak the Word of God loud and clear.

Bind the Devil Up

Satan is a thief (John 10:10) and he'll steal your vision if you let him. He'll tell you it's not going to come to pass. You've got to bind him up. If you're willing to do that, then God will bind him up. Whatever you bind on earth will be bound in heaven. (Matt. 16:19).

But after Satan is bound up, you have to have put action to your faith. Walk the floor and confess the opposite of what the devil is doing. Then when you get through confessing for about 30 minutes in English, spend another 30 minutes or longer praying in the Holy Ghost. Spend time praying in the Holy Ghost, building yourself up on your most holy faith, because holy faith sees no defeat.

But don't ever look at your vision through your natural eyes. Because your natural eyes will get you in trouble. Always look at a situation with the eyes of your spirit man.

If your business is going broke, go out in front of it and talk to it, and see success. Talk to it. People ask me: ''Do you talk to your businesses?'' Oh, yes! That's the reason I have nine successful ones.

You have to bind the devil up and speak to him. Satan will talk you out of what you have and what God wants you to do unless you spend time praying in the Holy Ghost to keep yourself built up.

If you keep your spirit built up by praying in the Holy Ghost, then you'll be able to recognize visions. Always remember that until you pick up something in your spirit, the Holy Ghost can never help you. If you don't study the Bible, you won't understand visions. You won't know what they mean.

If you haven't studied the Bible on visions, and you don't know anything about visions, if you don't know the emphasis the Bible places on visions, then you won't understand the importance of receiving a vision. If scriptures about visions are not on the inside of you, then you won't ever recognize or receive a vision from the Lord.

Study what the Bible says about visions. Give the Holy Spirit something to work with in your spirit where visions are concerned.

Let the Love of God Spill Out

The more you know God, the better you become. You become stronger. More of the love of God gets in you.

The better you know the Lord, the more the love of God will rise up in you. Let the love of God spill out. Just keep passing out tracts, knocking on doors, and casting out devils. Do those things, and you won't lose your vision. You'll never lose it.

Any church that does not reach out to its own town has lost its vision for lost souls. Such people have lost their vision. The Bible says that without a vision, the people perish. (Prov. 29:18). If you have received a vision of helping people on the foreign field — or wherever God wants you to go for Him — don't ever lose that vision for lost souls.

If you're going to go into the ministry, you'd better not lose the vision of helping people. Make yourself available to the Holy Ghost.

Pray Until the Fire Comes

Do you know what the fire of God does? The fire of God burns the chaff out of you. It burns out everything that's not supposed to be there.

How do you get baptized in the fire? By praying in tongues. Just get flat on your face before God and start praying in tongues. Pray for several hours. Ask the Holy Ghost to burn the chaff out of you. It'll hurt. I can promise you that. It'll feel like a burning sensation on the inside of you. But it will get rid of the chaff that's in you.

Let's say, for instance, that you have a hot temper you want to get rid of. Get flat on the floor and take authority over that spirit of temper that's making your family live in a little hell and causing you to feel ashamed after you go off on one of those temper rages.

Just take authority over it, in Jesus' name. Say:

"Spirit of temper, I break your power and I command you — go from me completely. Go from me, in Jesus' name. Lord, I want to be set free from the spirit of temper."

Then start praying in the Holy Ghost. Praying in tongues will get the mind of God for you. You asked to be free of temper. The Holy Ghost will do it for you. It's God's will for you to be free of temper. So ask for what you need. The Lord says that you have not because you ask not. (James 4:2). So bind up that spirit of temper, in Jesus' name, asking God to set you free. Then start praying in tongues, and keep on praying until you get beyond tongues.

You need to pray long enough to get beyond tongues. Most Christians don't do that. When the Holy Spirit gets you beyond tongues, He will take you over into the realm of groaning before the Lord. Then the fire of God will come and burn out of you everything that needs to be burned out. You won't be ashamed of the Gospel. You won't be ashamed of anything. You'll have patience. And you'll have peace.

In a Vision,
I Saw the Next Revival

In a vision several years ago, I saw the next revival come to earth.

This is what the Lord showed me in an open vision. I saw four winds coming from the east, west, north and south. All the four winds from the four corners of the earth met up in the sky head on and became one great big funnel, and the funnel began to come to the earth. Then the word of the Lord came to me, saying: "This is the way the revival will come to the earth. It will come like the wind from different directions. It will just come, and I am going to use young people as a great part to spread the revival."

What good are visions? Why do you need to understand them? A vision is God's window to the supernatural. A vision can warn you and expose Satan's plots so that you can pray to stop them from happening. A vision can guide you, instruct you, and set you free from bondage. A vision can get you ready for your ministry. God can add to your ministry through a vision. A vision can show you how God wants you to go out and act on His behalf to bring complete deliverance to people and to change things in their world.

Study what the Bible has to say about visions. Be open to receiving visions from the Lord. Through the blessing of visions, let the Lord have a chance to show you what he wants you to see — what part He wants you to play in the great revival I saw in my vision, the revival which is coming soon.

Other Books by Norvel Hayes

How To Live and Not Die

*The Winds of God
Bring Revival*

*God's Power Through
the Laying on of Hands*

The Blessing of Obedience

*Stand in the Gap
for Your Children*

*How To Get
Your Prayers Answered*

Endued With Power

Prostitute Faith

*The Number One Way
To Fight the Devil*

*Why You Should
Speak in Tongues*

What To Do for Healing

*How To Triumph
Over Sickness*

*Financial Dominion —
How To Take Charge
of Your Finances*

The Healing Handbook

*Rescuing Souls
From Hell —
Handbook for
Effective Soulwinning*

How To Cast Out Devils

Radical Christianity

*Secrets To Keeping
Your Faith Strong*

*Putting Your Angels
To Work*

Know Your Enemy

**Available from your local bookstore,
or by writing:**

Harrison House
P. O. Box 35035 • Tulsa, OK 74153

Norvel Hayes shares God's Word boldly and simply, with an enthusiasm that captures the heart of the hearer. He has learned through personal experience that God's Word can be effective in every area of life and that it will work for anyone who will believe it and apply it.

Norvel owns several businesses which function successfully despite the fact that he spends more than half his time away from the office, ministering the Gospel throughout the country. His obedience to God and his willingness to share his faith have taken him to a variety of places. He ministers in churches, seminars, conventions, colleges, prisons — anywhere the Spirit of God leads.

For a complete list of tapes and
books by Norvel Hayes, write:

Norvel Hayes
P. O. Box 1379
Cleveland, TN 37311

Please feel free to include your prayer requests and comments when you write.

In Canada contact:
Word Alive
P. O. Box 284
Niverville, Manitoba
CANADA R0A 1E0

For international sales in Europe,
contact:

Harrison House Europe
Belruptstrasse 42 A
A - 6900 Bregenz
AUSTRIA

The Harrison House Vision

Proclaiming the truth and the power
Of the Gospel of Jesus Christ
With excellence;

Challenging Christians to
Live victoriously,
Grow spiritually,
Know God intimately.